Witches in Art and Literature

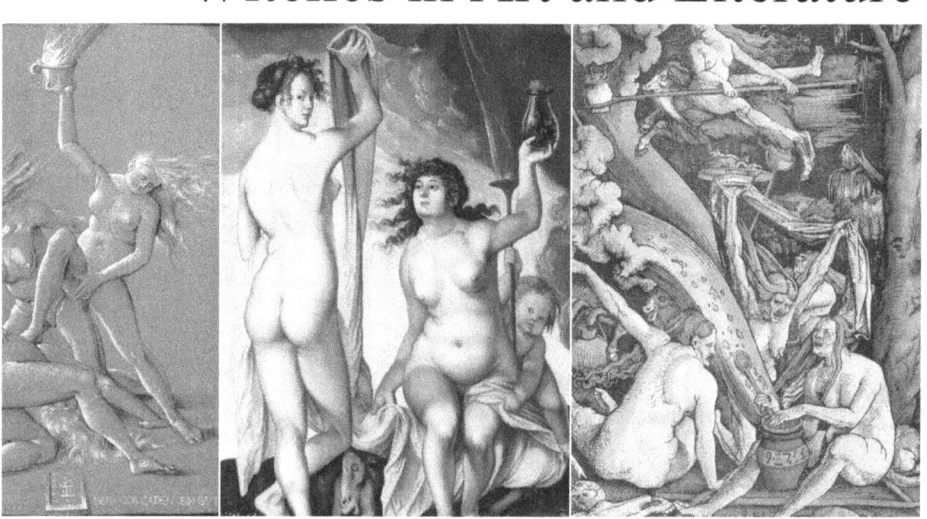

Edited by Lacey Belinda Smith

Contents

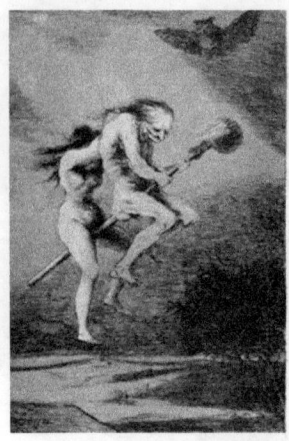

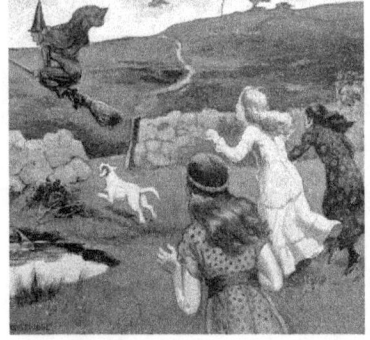

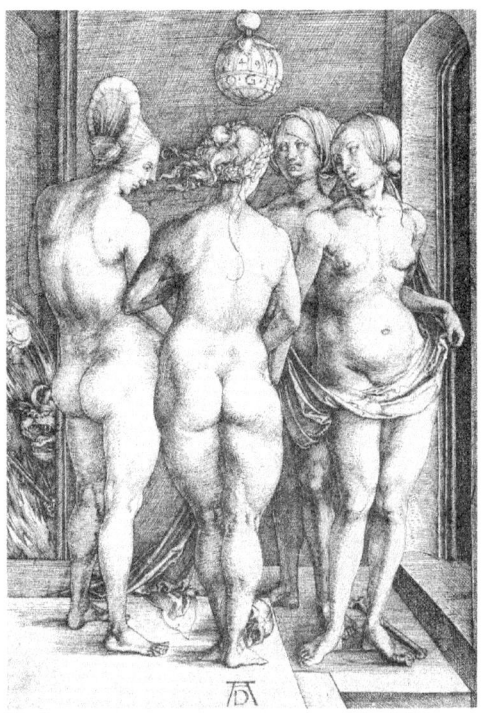

The Four Witches--Albrecht Durer-- 1497

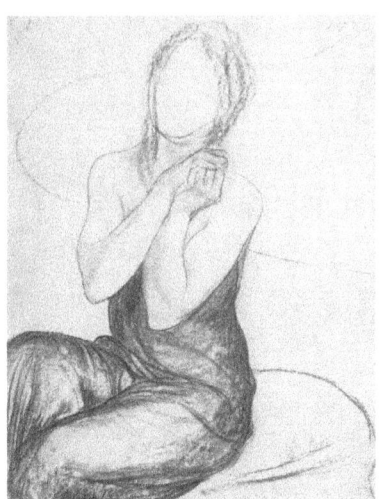

Kuzma Petrov-Vodkin--Drawing a picture of the Witch—1908

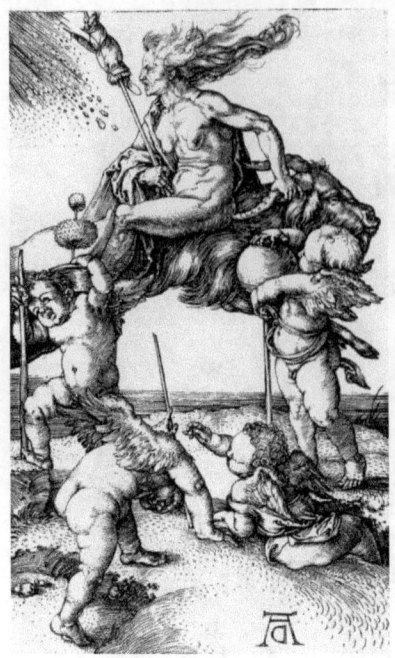

Albrecht Durer Witch Riding Backwards On A Goat--1500

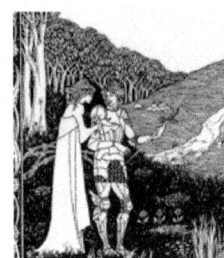

Aubrey Beardsley--Sir Launcelot and the Witch Hellawes

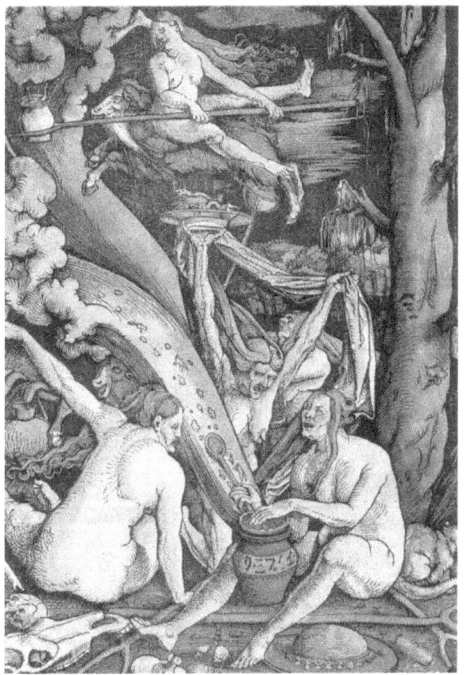

Hans Baldung--Witches--1508

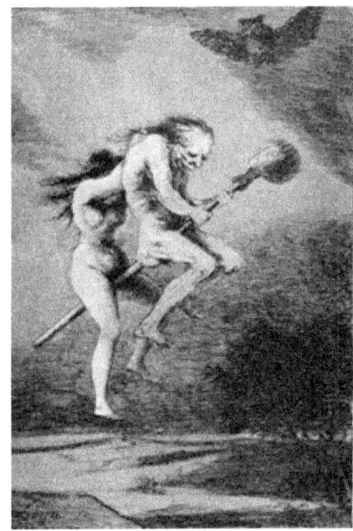

Pretty teacher-- Francisco Goya-- 1799

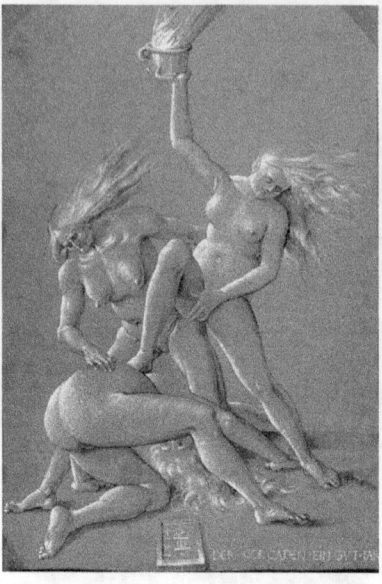

Hans Baldung—Witches--1514

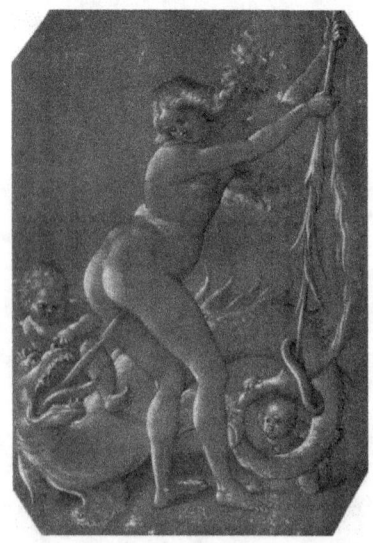

Hans Baldung--Standing witch with monster--1515

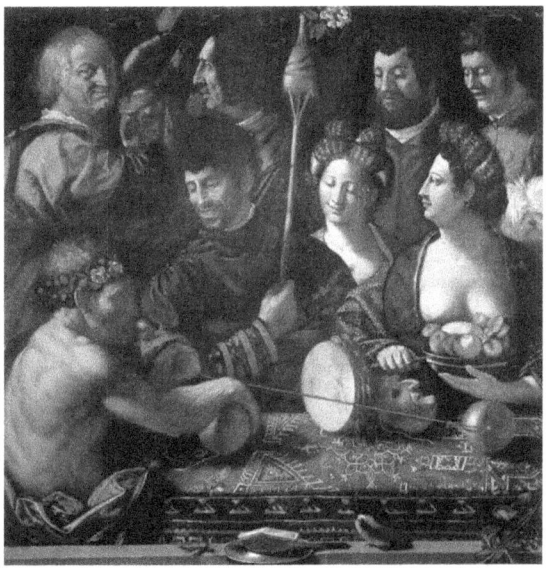

Dosso Dossi--Witchcraft (Allegory of Hercules)—1523

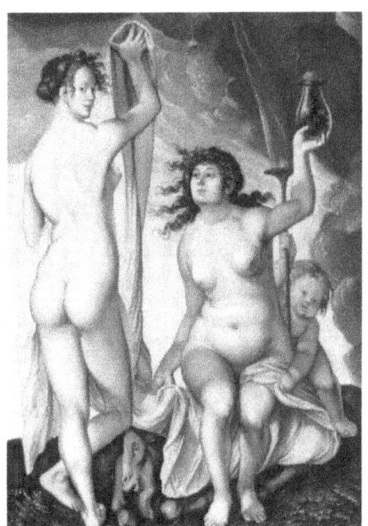

Two Witches--Hans Baldung --1523

The Witch of Atlas

Percy Bysshe Shelley

TO MARY (ON HER OBJECTING TO THE FOLLOWING POEM, UPON THE SCORE OF ITS CONTAINING NO HUMAN INTEREST).

1.

How, my dear Mary,—are you critic-bitten
(For vipers kill, though dead) by some review,
That you condemn these verses I have written,
Because they tell no story, false or true?
What, though no mice are caught by a young kitten, _5
May it not leap and play as grown cats do,
Till its claws come? Prithee, for this one time,
Content thee with a visionary rhyme.

2.

What hand would crush the silken-winged fly,
The youngest of inconstant April's minions, _10
Because it cannot climb the purest sky,
Where the swan sings, amid the sun's dominions?
Not thine. Thou knowest 'tis its doom to die,
When Day shall hide within her twilight pinions
The lucent eyes, and the eternal smile, _15
Serene as thine, which lent it life awhile.

3.

To thy fair feet a winged Vision came,
Whose date should have been longer than a day,
And o'er thy head did beat its wings for fame,
And in thy sight its fading plumes display; _20
The watery bow burned in the evening flame.
But the shower fell, the swift Sun went his way—
And that is dead.—O, let me not believe
That anything of mine is fit to live!

4.

Wordsworth informs us he was nineteen years _25
Considering and retouching Peter Bell;
Watering his laurels with the killing tears
Of slow, dull care, so that their roots to Hell
Might pierce, and their wide branches blot the spheres
Of Heaven, with dewy leaves and flowers; this well _30
May be, for Heaven and Earth conspire to foil
The over-busy gardener's blundering toil.

5.

My Witch indeed is not so sweet a creature
As Ruth or Lucy, whom his graceful praise
Clothes for our grandsons—but she matches Peter, _35
Though he took nineteen years, and she three days
In dressing. Light the vest of flowing metre
She wears; he, proud as dandy with his stays,
Has hung upon his wiry limbs a dress
Like King Lear's 'looped and windowed raggedness.' _40

6.

If you strip Peter, you will see a fellow
Scorched by Hell's hyperequatorial climate
Into a kind of a sulphureous yellow:
A lean mark, hardly fit to fling a rhyme at;
In shape a Scaramouch, in hue Othello. _45
If you unveil my Witch, no priest nor primate
Can shrive you of that sin,—if sin there be
In love, when it becomes idolatry.

THE WITCH OF ATLAS.

1.

Before those cruel Twins, whom at one birth
Incestuous Change bore to her father Time, _50
Error and Truth, had hunted from the Earth
All those bright natures which adorned its prime,
And left us nothing to believe in, worth
The pains of putting into learned rhyme,
A lady-witch there lived on Atlas' mountain _55
Within a cavern, by a secret fountain.

2.

Her mother was one of the Atlantides:
The all-beholding Sun had ne'er beholden
In his wide voyage o'er continents and seas
So fair a creature, as she lay enfolden _60
In the warm shadow of her loveliness;—
He kissed her with his beams, and made all golden
The chamber of gray rock in which she lay—
She, in that dream of joy, dissolved away.

3.

'Tis said, she first was changed into a vapour, _65
And then into a cloud, such clouds as flit,
Like splendour-winged moths about a taper,
Round the red west when the sun dies in it:
And then into a meteor, such as caper
On hill-tops when the moon is in a fit: _70
Then, into one of those mysterious stars
Which hide themselves between the Earth and Mars.

4.

Ten times the Mother of the Months had bent
Her bow beside the folding-star, and bidden
With that bright sign the billows to indent _75
The sea-deserted sand—like children chidden,
At her command they ever came and went—
Since in that cave a dewy splendour hidden
Took shape and motion: with the living form
Of this embodied Power, the cave grew warm. _80

5.

A lovely lady garmented in light
From her own beauty—deep her eyes, as are
Two openings of unfathomable night
Seen through a Temple's cloven roof—her hair
Dark—the dim brain whirls dizzy with delight. _85
Picturing her form; her soft smiles shone afar,
And her low voice was heard like love, and drew
All living things towards this wonder new.

6.

And first the spotted cameleopard came,
And then the wise and fearless elephant; _90

Then the sly serpent, in the golden flame
Of his own volumes intervolved;—all gaunt
And sanguine beasts her gentle looks made tame.
They drank before her at her sacred fount;
And every beast of beating heart grew bold, _95
Such gentleness and power even to behold.

    7.

The brinded lioness led forth her young,
That she might teach them how they should forego
Their inborn thirst of death; the pard unstrung
His sinews at her feet, and sought to know _100
With looks whose motions spoke without a tongue
How he might be as gentle as the doe.
The magic circle of her voice and eyes
All savage natures did imparadise.

    8.

And old Silenus, shaking a green stick _105
Of lilies, and the wood-gods in a crew
Came, blithe, as in the olive copses thick
Cicadae are, drunk with the noonday dew:
And Dryope and Faunus followed quick,
Teasing the God to sing them something new; _110
Till in this cave they found the lady lone,
Sitting upon a seat of emerald stone.

    9.

And universal Pan, 'tis said, was there,
And though none saw him,—through the adamant
Of the deep mountains, through the trackless air, _115
And through those living spirits, like a want,
He passed out of his everlasting lair
Where the quick heart of the great world doth pant,
And felt that wondrous lady all alone,—
And she felt him, upon her emerald throne. _120

    10.

And every nymph of stream and spreading tree,
And every shepherdess of Ocean's flocks,
Who drives her white waves over the green sea,
And Ocean with the brine on his gray locks,
And quaint Priapus with his company, _125

All came, much wondering how the enwombed rocks
Could have brought forth so beautiful a birth;—
Her love subdued their wonder and their mirth.

11.

The herdsmen and the mountain maidens came,
And the rude kings of pastoral Garamant— _130
Their spirits shook within them, as a flame
Stirred by the air under a cavern gaunt:
Pigmies, and Polyphemes, by many a name,
Centaurs, and Satyrs, and such shapes as haunt
Wet clefts,—and lumps neither alive nor dead, _135
Dog-headed, bosom-eyed, and bird-footed.

12.

For she was beautiful—her beauty made
The bright world dim, and everything beside
Seemed like the fleeting image of a shade:
No thought of living spirit could abide, _140
Which to her looks had ever been betrayed,
On any object in the world so wide,
On any hope within the circling skies,
But on her form, and in her inmost eyes.

13.

Which when the lady knew, she took her spindle _145
And twined three threads of fleecy mist, and three
Long lines of light, such as the dawn may kindle
The clouds and waves and mountains with; and she
As many star-beams, ere their lamps could dwindle
In the belated moon, wound skilfully; _150
And with these threads a subtle veil she wove—
A shadow for the splendour of her love.

14.

The deep recesses of her odorous dwelling
Were stored with magic treasures—sounds of air,
Which had the power all spirits of compelling, _155
Folded in cells of crystal silence there;
Such as we hear in youth, and think the feeling
Will never die—yet ere we are aware,
The feeling and the sound are fled and gone,
And the regret they leave remains alone. _160

15.

And there lay Visions swift, and sweet, and quaint,
Each in its thin sheath, like a chrysalis,
Some eager to burst forth, some weak and faint
With the soft burthen of intensest bliss.
It was its work to bear to many a saint _165
Whose heart adores the shrine which holiest is,
Even Love's:—and others white, green, gray, and black,
And of all shapes—and each was at her beck.

16.

And odours in a kind of aviary
Of ever-blooming Eden-trees she kept, _170
Clipped in a floating net, a love-sick Fairy
Had woven from dew-beams while the moon yet slept;
As bats at the wired window of a dairy,
They beat their vans; and each was an adept,
When loosed and missioned, making wings of winds, _175
To stir sweet thoughts or sad, in destined minds.

17.

And liquors clear and sweet, whose healthful might
Could medicine the sick soul to happy sleep,
And change eternal death into a night
Of glorious dreams—or if eyes needs must weep, _180
Could make their tears all wonder and delight,
She in her crystal vials did closely keep:
If men could drink of those clear vials, 'tis said
The living were not envied of the dead.

18.

Her cave was stored with scrolls of strange device, _185
The works of some Saturnian Archimage,
Which taught the expiations at whose price
Men from the Gods might win that happy age
Too lightly lost, redeeming native vice;
And which might quench the Earth-consuming rage _190
Of gold and blood—till men should live and move
Harmonious as the sacred stars above;

19.

And how all things that seem untameable,
Not to be checked and not to be confined,

Obey the spells of Wisdom's wizard skill; _195
Time, earth, and fire—the ocean and the wind,
And all their shapes—and man's imperial will;
And other scrolls whose writings did unbind
The inmost lore of Love—let the profane
Tremble to ask what secrets they contain. _200

   20.

And wondrous works of substances unknown,
To which the enchantment of her father's power
Had changed those ragged blocks of savage stone,
Were heaped in the recesses of her bower;
Carved lamps and chalices, and vials which shone _205
In their own golden beams—each like a flower,
Out of whose depth a fire-fly shakes his light
Under a cypress in a starless night.

   21.

At first she lived alone in this wild home,
And her own thoughts were each a minister, _210
Clothing themselves, or with the ocean foam,
Or with the wind, or with the speed of fire,
To work whatever purposes might come
Into her mind; such power her mighty Sire
Had girt them with, whether to fly or run, _215
Through all the regions which he shines upon.

   22.

The Ocean-nymphs and Hamadryades,
Oreads and Naiads, with long weedy locks,
Offered to do her bidding through the seas,
Under the earth, and in the hollow rocks, _220
And far beneath the matted roots of trees,
And in the gnarled heart of stubborn oaks,
So they might live for ever in the light
Of her sweet presence—each a satellite.

   23.

'This may not be,' the wizard maid replied; _225
'The fountains where the Naiades bedew
Their shining hair, at length are drained and dried;
The solid oaks forget their strength, and strew
Their latest leaf upon the mountains wide;

The boundless ocean like a drop of dew _230
Will be consumed—the stubborn centre must
Be scattered, like a cloud of summer dust.

    24.

'And ye with them will perish, one by one;—
If I must sigh to think that this shall be,
If I must weep when the surviving Sun _235
Shall smile on your decay—oh, ask not me
To love you till your little race is run;
I cannot die as ye must—over me
Your leaves shall glance—the streams in which ye dwell
Shall be my paths henceforth, and so—farewell!'— _240

    25.

She spoke and wept:—the dark and azure well
Sparkled beneath the shower of her bright tears,
And every little circlet where they fell
Flung to the cavern-roof inconstant spheres
And intertangled lines of light:—a knell _245
Of sobbing voices came upon her ears
From those departing Forms, o'er the serene
Of the white streams and of the forest green.

    26.

All day the wizard lady sate aloof,
Spelling out scrolls of dread antiquity, _250
Under the cavern's fountain-lighted roof;
Or broidering the pictured poesy
Of some high tale upon her growing woof,
Which the sweet splendour of her smiles could dye
In hues outshining heaven—and ever she _255
Added some grace to the wrought poesy.

    27.

While on her hearth lay blazing many a piece
Of sandal wood, rare gums, and cinnamon;
Men scarcely know how beautiful fire is—
Each flame of it is as a precious stone _260
Dissolved in ever-moving light, and this
Belongs to each and all who gaze upon.
The Witch beheld it not, for in her hand
She held a woof that dimmed the burning brand.

28.
This lady never slept, but lay in trance _265
All night within the fountain—as in sleep.
Its emerald crags glowed in her beauty's glance;
Through the green splendour of the water deep
She saw the constellations reel and dance
Like fire-flies—and withal did ever keep _270
The tenour of her contemplations calm,
With open eyes, closed feet, and folded palm.

29.
And when the whirlwinds and the clouds descended
From the white pinnacles of that cold hill,
She passed at dewfall to a space extended, _275
Where in a lawn of flowering asphodel
Amid a wood of pines and cedars blended,
There yawned an inextinguishable well
Of crimson fire—full even to the brim,
And overflowing all the margin trim. _280

30.
Within the which she lay when the fierce war
Of wintry winds shook that innocuous liquor
In many a mimic moon and bearded star
O'er woods and lawns;—the serpent heard it flicker
In sleep, and dreaming still, he crept afar— _285
And when the windless snow descended thicker
Than autumn leaves, she watched it as it came
Melt on the surface of the level flame.

31.
She had a boat, which some say Vulcan wrought
For Venus, as the chariot of her star; _290
But it was found too feeble to be fraught
With all the ardours in that sphere which are,
And so she sold it, and Apollo bought
And gave it to this daughter: from a car
Changed to the fairest and the lightest boat _295
Which ever upon mortal stream did float.

32.
And others say, that, when but three hours old,
The first-born Love out of his cradle lept,

And clove dun Chaos with his wings of gold,
And like a horticultural adept, _300
Stole a strange seed, and wrapped it up in mould,
And sowed it in his mother's star, and kept
Watering it all the summer with sweet dew,
And with his wings fanning it as it grew.

33.

The plant grew strong and green, the snowy flower _305
Fell, and the long and gourd-like fruit began
To turn the light and dew by inward power
To its own substance; woven tracery ran
Of light firm texture, ribbed and branching, o'er
The solid rind, like a leaf's veined fan— _310
Of which Love scooped this boat—and with soft motion
Piloted it round the circumfluous ocean.

34.

This boat she moored upon her fount, and lit
A living spirit within all its frame,
Breathing the soul of swiftness into it. _315
Couched on the fountain like a panther tame,
One of the twain at Evan's feet that sit—
Or as on Vesta's sceptre a swift flame—
Or on blind Homer's heart a winged thought,—
In joyous expectation lay the boat. _320

35.

Then by strange art she kneaded fire and snow
Together, tempering the repugnant mass
With liquid love—all things together grow
Through which the harmony of love can pass;
And a fair Shape out of her hands did flow— _325
A living Image, which did far surpass
In beauty that bright shape of vital stone
Which drew the heart out of Pygmalion.

36.

A sexless thing it was, and in its growth
It seemed to have developed no defect _330
Of either sex, yet all the grace of both,—
In gentleness and strength its limbs were decked;
The bosom swelled lightly with its full youth,

The countenance was such as might select
Some artist that his skill should never die, _335
Imaging forth such perfect purity.

   37.

From its smooth shoulders hung two rapid wings,
Fit to have borne it to the seventh sphere,
Tipped with the speed of liquid lightenings,
Dyed in the ardours of the atmosphere: _340
She led her creature to the boiling springs
Where the light boat was moored, and said: 'Sit here!'
And pointed to the prow, and took her seat
Beside the rudder, with opposing feet.

   38.

And down the streams which clove those mountains vast, _345
Around their inland islets, and amid
The panther-peopled forests whose shade cast
Darkness and odours, and a pleasure hid
In melancholy gloom, the pinnace passed;
By many a star-surrounded pyramid _350
Of icy crag cleaving the purple sky,
And caverns yawning round unfathomably.

   39.

The silver noon into that winding dell,
With slanted gleam athwart the forest tops,
Tempered like golden evening, feebly fell; _355
A green and glowing light, like that which drops
From folded lilies in which glow-worms dwell,
When Earth over her face Night's mantle wraps;
Between the severed mountains lay on high,
Over the stream, a narrow rift of sky. _360

   40.

And ever as she went, the Image lay
With folded wings and unawakened eyes;
And o'er its gentle countenance did play
The busy dreams, as thick as summer flies,
Chasing the rapid smiles that would not stay, _365
And drinking the warm tears, and the sweet sighs
Inhaling, which, with busy murmur vain,
They had aroused from that full heart and brain.

41.

And ever down the prone vale, like a cloud
Upon a stream of wind, the pinnace went: _370
Now lingering on the pools, in which abode
The calm and darkness of the deep content
In which they paused; now o'er the shallow road
Of white and dancing waters, all besprent
With sand and polished pebbles:—mortal boat _375
In such a shallow rapid could not float.

42.

And down the earthquaking cataracts which shiver
Their snow-like waters into golden air,
Or under chasms unfathomable ever
Sepulchre them, till in their rage they tear _380
A subterranean portal for the river,
It fled—the circling sunbows did upbear
Its fall down the hoar precipice of spray,
Lighting it far upon its lampless way.

43.

And when the wizard lady would ascend _385
The labyrinths of some many-winding vale,
Which to the inmost mountain upward tend—
She called 'Hermaphroditus!'—and the pale
And heavy hue which slumber could extend
Over its lips and eyes, as on the gale _390
A rapid shadow from a slope of grass,
Into the darkness of the stream did pass.

44.

And it unfurled its heaven-coloured pinions,
With stars of fire spotting the stream below;
And from above into the Sun's dominions _395
Flinging a glory, like the golden glow
In which Spring clothes her emerald-winged minions,
All interwoven with fine feathery snow
And moonlight splendour of intensest rime,
With which frost paints the pines in winter time. _400

45.

And then it winnowed the Elysian air
Which ever hung about that lady bright,

With its aethereal vans—and speeding there,
Like a star up the torrent of the night,
Or a swift eagle in the morning glare _405
Breasting the whirlwind with impetuous flight,
The pinnace, oared by those enchanted wings,
Clove the fierce streams towards their upper springs.

46.

The water flashed, like sunlight by the prow
Of a noon-wandering meteor flung to Heaven; _410
The still air seemed as if its waves did flow
In tempest down the mountains; loosely driven
The lady's radiant hair streamed to and fro:
Beneath, the billows having vainly striven
Indignant and impetuous, roared to feel _415
The swift and steady motion of the keel.

47.

Or, when the weary moon was in the wane,
Or in the noon of interlunar night,
The lady-witch in visions could not chain
Her spirit; but sailed forth under the light _420
Of shooting stars, and bade extend amain
Its storm-outspeeding wings, the Hermaphrodite;
She to the Austral waters took her way,
Beyond the fabulous Thamondocana,—

48.

Where, like a meadow which no scythe has shaven, _425
Which rain could never bend, or whirl-blast shake,
With the Antarctic constellations paven,
Canopus and his crew, lay the Austral lake—
There she would build herself a windless haven
Out of the clouds whose moving turrets make _430
The bastions of the storm, when through the sky
The spirits of the tempest thundered by:

49.

A haven beneath whose translucent floor
The tremulous stars sparkled unfathomably,
And around which the solid vapours hoar, _435
Based on the level waters, to the sky
Lifted their dreadful crags, and like a shore

Of wintry mountains, inaccessibly
Hemmed in with rifts and precipices gray,
And hanging crags, many a cove and bay. _440
   50.
And whilst the outer lake beneath the lash
Of the wind's scourge, foamed like a wounded thing,
And the incessant hail with stony clash
Ploughed up the waters, and the flagging wing
Of the roused cormorant in the lightning flash _445
Looked like the wreck of some wind-wandering
Fragment of inky thunder-smoke—this haven
Was as a gem to copy Heaven engraven,—
   51.
On which that lady played her many pranks,
Circling the image of a shooting star, _450
Even as a tiger on Hydaspes' banks
Outspeeds the antelopes which speediest are,
In her light boat; and many quips and cranks
She played upon the water, till the car
Of the late moon, like a sick matron wan, _455
To journey from the misty east began.
   52.
And then she called out of the hollow turrets
Of those high clouds, white, golden and vermilion,
The armies of her ministering spirits—
In mighty legions, million after million, _460
They came, each troop emblazoning its merits
On meteor flags; and many a proud pavilion
Of the intertexture of the atmosphere
They pitched upon the plain of the calm mere.
   53.
They framed the imperial tent of their great Queen _465
Of woven exhalations, underlaid
With lambent lightning-fire, as may be seen
A dome of thin and open ivory inlaid
With crimson silk—cressets from the serene
Hung there, and on the water for her tread _470
A tapestry of fleece-like mist was strewn,
Dyed in the beams of the ascending moon.

54.

And on a throne o'erlaid with starlight, caught
Upon those wandering isles of aery dew,
Which highest shoals of mountain shipwreck not, _475
She sate, and heard all that had happened new
Between the earth and moon, since they had brought
The last intelligence—and now she grew
Pale as that moon, lost in the watery night—
And now she wept, and now she laughed outright. _480

55.

These were tame pleasures; she would often climb
The steepest ladder of the crudded rack
Up to some beaked cape of cloud sublime,
And like Arion on the dolphin's back
Ride singing through the shoreless air;—oft-time _485
Following the serpent lightning's winding track,
She ran upon the platforms of the wind,
And laughed to hear the fire-balls roar behind.

56.

And sometimes to those streams of upper air
Which whirl the earth in its diurnal round, _490
She would ascend, and win the spirits there
To let her join their chorus. Mortals found
That on those days the sky was calm and fair,
And mystic snatches of harmonious sound
Wandered upon the earth where'er she passed, _495
And happy thoughts of hope, too sweet to last.

57.

But her choice sport was, in the hours of sleep,
To glide adown old Nilus, where he threads
Egypt and Aethiopia, from the steep
Of utmost Axume, until he spreads, _500
Like a calm flock of silver-fleeced sheep,
His waters on the plain: and crested heads
Of cities and proud temples gleam amid,
And many a vapour-belted pyramid.

58.

By Moeris and the Mareotid lakes, _505
Strewn with faint blooms like bridal chamber floors,

Where naked boys bridling tame water-snakes,
Or charioteering ghastly alligators,
Had left on the sweet waters mighty wakes
Of those huge forms—within the brazen doors _510
Of the great Labyrinth slept both boy and beast,
Tired with the pomp of their Osirian feast.

  59.

And where within the surface of the river
The shadows of the massy temples lie,
And never are erased—but tremble ever _515
Like things which every cloud can doom to die,
Through lotus-paven canals, and wheresoever
The works of man pierced that serenest sky
With tombs, and towers, and fanes, 'twas her delight
To wander in the shadow of the night. _520

  60.

With motion like the spirit of that wind
Whose soft step deepens slumber, her light feet
Passed through the peopled haunts of humankind.
Scattering sweet visions from her presence sweet,
Through fane, and palace-court, and labyrinth mined _525
With many a dark and subterranean street
Under the Nile, through chambers high and deep
She passed, observing mortals in their sleep.

  61.

A pleasure sweet doubtless it was to see
Mortals subdued in all the shapes of sleep. _530
Here lay two sister twins in infancy;
There, a lone youth who in his dreams did weep;
Within, two lovers linked innocently
In their loose locks which over both did creep
Like ivy from one stem;—and there lay calm _535
Old age with snow-bright hair and folded palm.

  62.

But other troubled forms of sleep she saw,
Not to be mirrored in a holy song—
Distortions foul of supernatural awe,
And pale imaginings of visioned wrong; _540
And all the code of Custom's lawless law

Written upon the brows of old and young:
'This,' said the wizard maiden, 'is the strife
Which stirs the liquid surface of man's life.'

63.

And little did the sight disturb her soul.— _545
We, the weak mariners of that wide lake
Where'er its shores extend or billows roll,
Our course unpiloted and starless make
O'er its wild surface to an unknown goal:—
But she in the calm depths her way could take, _550
Where in bright bowers immortal forms abide
Beneath the weltering of the restless tide.

64.

And she saw princes couched under the glow
Of sunlike gems; and round each temple-court
In dormitories ranged, row after row, _555
She saw the priests asleep—all of one sort—
For all were educated to be so.—
The peasants in their huts, and in the port
The sailors she saw cradled on the waves,
And the dead lulled within their dreamless graves. _560

65.

And all the forms in which those spirits lay
Were to her sight like the diaphanous
Veils, in which those sweet ladies oft array
Their delicate limbs, who would conceal from us
Only their scorn of all concealment: they _565
Move in the light of their own beauty thus.
But these and all now lay with sleep upon them,
And little thought a Witch was looking on them.

66.

She, all those human figures breathing there,
Beheld as living spirits—to her eyes _570
The naked beauty of the soul lay bare,
And often through a rude and worn disguise
She saw the inner form most bright and fair—
And then she had a charm of strange device,
Which, murmured on mute lips with tender tone, _575
Could make that spirit mingle with her own.

67.

Alas! Aurora, what wouldst thou have given
For such a charm when Tithon became gray?
Or how much, Venus, of thy silver heaven
Wouldst thou have yielded, ere Proserpina _580
Had half (oh! why not all?) the debt forgiven
Which dear Adonis had been doomed to pay,
To any witch who would have taught you it?
The Heliad doth not know its value yet.

68.

'Tis said in after times her spirit free _585
Knew what love was, and felt itself alone—
But holy Dian could not chaster be
Before she stooped to kiss Endymion,
Than now this lady—like a sexless bee
Tasting all blossoms, and confined to none, _590
Among those mortal forms, the wizard-maiden
Passed with an eye serene and heart unladen.

69.

To those she saw most beautiful, she gave
Strange panacea in a crystal bowl:—
They drank in their deep sleep of that sweet wave, _595
And lived thenceforward as if some control,
Mightier than life, were in them; and the grave
Of such, when death oppressed the weary soul,
Was as a green and overarching bower
Lit by the gems of many a starry flower. _600

70.

For on the night when they were buried, she
Restored the embalmers' ruining, and shook
The light out of the funeral lamps, to be
A mimic day within that deathy nook;
And she unwound the woven imagery _605
Of second childhood's swaddling bands, and took
The coffin, its last cradle, from its niche,
And threw it with contempt into a ditch.

71.

And there the body lay, age after age.
Mute, breathing, beating, warm, and undecaying, _610

Like one asleep in a green hermitage,
With gentle smiles about its eyelids playing,
And living in its dreams beyond the rage
Of death or life; while they were still arraying
In liveries ever new, the rapid, blind _615
And fleeting generations of mankind.

72.

And she would write strange dreams upon the brain
Of those who were less beautiful, and make
All harsh and crooked purposes more vain
Than in the desert is the serpent's wake _620
Which the sand covers—all his evil gain
The miser in such dreams would rise and shake
Into a beggar's lap;—the lying scribe
Would his own lies betray without a bribe.

73.

The priests would write an explanation full, _625
Translating hieroglyphics into Greek,
How the God Apis really was a bull,
And nothing more; and bid the herald stick
The same against the temple doors, and pull
The old cant down; they licensed all to speak _630
Whate'er they thought of hawks, and cats, and geese,
By pastoral letters to each diocese.

74.

The king would dress an ape up in his crown
And robes, and seat him on his glorious seat,
And on the right hand of the sunlike throne _635
Would place a gaudy mock-bird to repeat
The chatterings of the monkey.—Every one
Of the prone courtiers crawled to kiss the feet
Of their great Emperor, when the morning came,
And kissed—alas, how many kiss the same! _640

75.

The soldiers dreamed that they were blacksmiths, and
Walked out of quarters in somnambulism;
Round the red anvils you might see them stand
Like Cyclopses in Vulcan's sooty abysm,
Beating their swords to ploughshares;—in a band _645

The gaolers sent those of the liberal schism
Free through the streets of Memphis, much, I wis,
To the annoyance of king Amasis.

    76.

And timid lovers who had been so coy,
They hardly knew whether they loved or not, _650
Would rise out of their rest, and take sweet joy,
To the fulfilment of their inmost thought;
And when next day the maiden and the boy
Met one another, both, like sinners caught,
Blushed at the thing which each believed was done _655
Only in fancy—till the tenth moon shone;

    77.

And then the Witch would let them take no ill:
Of many thousand schemes which lovers find,
The Witch found one,—and so they took their fill
Of happiness in marriage warm and kind. _660
Friends who, by practice of some envious skill,
Were torn apart—a wide wound, mind from mind!—
She did unite again with visions clear
Of deep affection and of truth sincere.

    80.

These were the pranks she played among the cities _665
Of mortal men, and what she did to Sprites
And Gods, entangling them in her sweet ditties
To do her will, and show their subtle sleights,
I will declare another time; for it is
A tale more fit for the weird winter nights _670
Than for these garish summer days, when we
Scarcely believe much more than we can see.

The Witch Hypnotizer

Zena A. Maher

CHAPTER I.

Let there be light. Genesis i, 3.

Let your light so shine before men, that they may see your good works, and glorify your Father which is in Heaven. Matthew v, 16.

In the world of imagination many Witches have lived and died since the one of whose existence and wonders I am about to relate, came into prominence.

She lived quite alone in a little cottage on the outskirts of a large city in America, of course, and why should not the free soil produce all sorts when it is the dumping ground for all creation?

Alone, with the exception of her dog and several cages of canaries which, by the way, were a new departure in the line of pets, for the old-time Witches were supposed to favor cats and parrots, she commanded the respect of all, but there was something so very peculiar about her that some of her more superstitious neighbors looked upon this woman as a kind of good Witch.

There was nothing remarkable about her personal appearance and the peculiarity was not visibly noticeable. It was nothing tangible, but an indescribable something which gave her influence over other minds, to bend them to her will.

Every one felt this more or less in her presence; a giving up of pet hobbies, even, to her ideas, which fortunately were very liberal.

There was that also about her sympathetic nature which invited confidence, and many who were not given to complaining found themselves, they hardly knew why, telling her their secret sorrows.

For years this Witch or woman was herself unconscious of this power, but when she fully realized it, her work to her conscientious heart was laid out, and that must be in doing all the good possible through this genius that was hers.

She had always endeavored to do her best, ever ready to lend a helping hand to any one in trouble.

CHAPTER II.

While attending to her birds one morning, the Witch was interrupted by a knock at the door and a summons from one of her neighbors, who had sent a child to ask if this good soul would come over.

Yes, she would be there directly.

Donning her sombre colored bonnet and shawl the Witch started for her neighbor's. The unhappy little woman craved sympathy, and had sent for her who knew so well how to render it.

She told the oft-repeated story of a drunkard's wife. Her husband had left home the previous evening and had not returned, and after these prolonged sprees she feared his coming, who was the kindest of men when himself, but very savage when under the influence of liquor. Then, too, she was afraid that he would lose his position, which his employer had threatened if he did not attend to work better.

The Witch told her to be of good cheer; that all would be well with her yet.

She looked at the shabby furniture and still shabbier clothing of the children. This family had once been in comfortable circumstances, but were brought to this state of poverty through intemperance, the prevailing evil.

For the drunkard and the glutton shall come to poverty. Proverbs, xxiii, 21.

And yet how much good these beverages might do if used in moderation, but too many are with this, like all their other appetites over which they have no control. The mind should be made to strive harder after the knowledge of God in order to subdue these carnal desires.

For they that are after the flesh do mind the things of the flesh; but they that are after the Spirit, the things of the Spirit.

For to be carnally minded is death; but to be spiritually minded is life and peace.

Because the carnal mind is enmity against God; for it is not subject to the law of God, neither indeed can be.

So then they that are in the flesh cannot please God.

As many as are led by the Spirit of God, they are the sons of God. Romans viii, 5, 6, 7, 8, 14.

Woe unto them that rise up early in the morning, that they may follow strong drink, that continue until night, till wine inflame them!

Woe unto them that are mighty to drink wine, and men of strength to mingle strong drink. Isaiah v, 11, 22.

He that soweth to his flesh shall of the flesh reap corruption; but he that soweth to the Spirit shall of the Spirit reap life everlasting. Galatians vi. 8.

All things indeed are pure; but it is evil for that man who eateth with offense.

It is good neither to eat flesh, nor to drink wine, nor anything whereby thy brother stumbleth, or is offended, or is made weak. Romans xiv, 20, 21.

Whilst we are at home in the body, we are absent from the Lord. II Corinthians v, 6.

Be not drunk with wine wherein is excess; but be filled with the Spirit. Ephesians v, 18.

Walk in the Spirit and ye shall not fulfill the lust of the flesh. Galatians v, 16.

Denying ungodliness and worldly lusts, we should live soberly, righteously and godly in this present world. Titus ii, 12.

About midday this fallen image of God came home partially sobered and ferocious as a wild animal. The Witch mentally compared man with beast and gave her dog the preference.

He had commenced his wicked profanity, when a hand was laid on his arm and reproachful eyes looked into his.

Wine is a mocker, strong drink is raging; and whoever is deceived thereby is not wise. Proverbs xx, 1.

God created man in his own image. Genesis i, 27.

Know ye not that ye are the temple of God, and that the Spirit of God dwelleth in you?

If any man defile the temple of God, him shall God destroy; for the temple of God is holy, which temple ye are. I Corinthians iii, 16, 17.

After this he sat quietly for a long time apparently lost in thought; then this truly penitent one arose, stood beside his wife and vowed that in future he would be a better man, and their home should be happy as in the old days before this false friend took possession.

Tears of happiness were streaming from the little woman's eyes, and our Witch withdrew, thanking God in her heart for this power he had given her.

31

CHAPTER III.

On reaching home she found a neighbor waiting outside, who entered with her, in the meantime pouring into the ever sympathetic ears her trouble.

She was bewailing over the downfall of her boy who heretofore had been exceptionally dutiful, invariably spending his evening at home, but of late all was changed. He had contracted the card disease with all its adherent vices, which was rapidly developing into a mania. His salary, which was the home support, was being sacrificed on the gambling altar.

Here was more work. The only son and mainstay of a widowed mother fast going to ruin. Yes, something must be done.

Early the following evening the Witch made it her business to pay a visit to the widow about tea time. The son was hurriedly finishing his meal preparatory to starting out for the night, when somehow he changed his mind and stayed at home instead, and our friend, the Witch, knew that in future he would have sufficient strength of will to pass by his old haunt and on home to his waiting loving mother with his earnings in his pocket, which meant more home comforts, more books and evening reading, and happiness to both.

Turn not to the right hand nor to the left; remove thy foot from evil. Proverbs, iv. 27.

The Witch went home well satisfied with her day's work, and that night thought and planned for the good of humanity. Why not venture further into a wider range for action?

She might peddle her songbirds from door to door, and in this capacity gain access into houses where she could more readily acquaint herself with those in need of her assistance.

CHAPTER IV.

The next morning our Witch opened her Bible and read as she was wont to do before any new undertaking. Her eyes rested on these lines:

If ye then, being evil, know how to give good gifts unto your children, how much more shall your Heavenly Father give the Holy Spirit to them that ask him? Luke xi, 13.

She knelt and prayed long and earnestly for an abundance of this Holy Spirit to guide and help her. She took her birds and started out.

I will put my spirit within you, and cause you to walk in my statutes, and ye shall keep my judgments and do them. Ezekiel xxxvi, 27.

Her first stopping place was at a dwelling that stood back some little distance from the street and was surrounded by flowers.

What drew her attention most was the appearance of a little child whose innocent face reminded her that purity still existed. She entered the grounds and rang the bell.

A young woman opened the door and kindly invited her in. The Witch made some remark about the pretty boy outside, when she saw an expression of pain flit over the lady's face. Something wrong here, she thought.

Yes, the child was hers; she had loved not wisely but too well, Her betrayer, a prosperous business man who was as yet unmarried, was allowed to move in the very best of society, but the finger of scorn was pointed at her from all sides.

She was the only daughter of parents who thought very fondly of their lovable grandchild, still felt keenly the disgrace that had been brought upon the hitherto spotless family name.

Does the seventh commandment demand more obedience from one sex than the other? It reads as if it was spoken to both alike. Our Witch learned the man's name and business address, and departed.

CHAPTER V.

She was so in sympathy with this family that she felt in a hurry to get to work, and so signalled a passing car to stop, and entered. It was well filled, but two seats remaining unoccupied she seated herself in one of them.

Presently a little colored girl came in and took the other. A high-bred dame sitting next elevated her aristocratic nose and pulled her skirts aside as if fearing contamination.

Hear ye, and give ear; be not proud; for the Lord hath spoken. Jeremiah xiii, 15.

There is a generation, O how lofty are their eyes! Proverbs xxx, 13.

Behold, I am against thee, O thou most proud, saith the Lord God of Hosts. Jeremiah 1, 31.

Every one that is proud in heart is an abomination to the Lord. Proverbs xvi, 5.

I will cause the arrogancy of the proud to cease, and will lay low the haughtiness of the terrible. Isaiah xiii, 11.

The lofty looks of man shall be humbled, and the haughtiness of men shall be bowed down. Isaiah ii, 11.

Why draw this color line so tightly? What of this outer covering? Have not these people immortal souls which may be white as the whitest; and in many cases, brilliant talents?

The Witch remembered a circumstance where a king of oratory, holding a high official position, was debarred from sitting at table with a ship's crew on account of this same color, which was only a heavier shading; and is not all creation a matter of shadow and coloring?

And hath made of one blood all nations of men for to dwell on all the face of the earth. Acts xvii, 26.

A shabbily dressed woman came in. The stamp of labor was on her gloveless hands, and she looked weary, indeed. But no attention was paid her whatever.

Then came two flashily attired females. No less than five gentlemen arose to offer seats. Were they more in need of rest than this poor laboring woman?

Ah, well! perhaps they were more heavily burdened with their follies than she with her cares.

For once the Witch was too busy with many thoughts to concentrate her mind on any individual in particular, and passed on and out of the car to finish her day's work.

CHAPTER VI.

She went in to a business establishment and made her way to the office. The proprietor, a busy man of the world, was at his desk. He looked in surprise at the cage of birds; a rather unusual place, certainly, to attempt the sale of a bird, the business house of a man without family.

"I have no use for pets myself, and have no one to give them to."

No one? Then memory stirred; he thought of the one whom he had so cruelly wronged, and of his innocent child in disgrace. Why were these new and better impulses taking possession of his mind? He did not know, but the Witch did.

She saw the result of her work a few days later when his marriage notice was published in the paper. Another family put to rights.

CHAPTER VII.

Next, a respectable looking place that might belong to the occupants, for there was not that unkempt appearance about it that is peculiar to rented property.

Our Witch opened the gate and went in. A scowling woman came to the door who looked daggers at the unwelcome peddler, and said she would not have one of those noisy birds in the house.

About this time her tired-looking husband came home from work, and judging from the tirade of abuse heaped upon him, it was evident that she certainly would not tolerate any noise about the premises that she could not make herself.

It was only a matter of time when this quiet, hard-working man would tire of his home life. Husbands with such life partners are not so much to blame if they do prefer the company of other women, the gambling dens and saloons, or any place rather than their homes.

It is better to dwell in a corner of the housetop than with a brawling woman in a wide house. Proverbs xxi, 9.

How many wives, instead of trying to make home attractive, drive happiness away with their cruel tongues?

Who have said with our tongue will we prevail; our lips are our own who is lord over us? Psalms xii, 4.

Hold thy tongue. Amos vi, 10.

The tongue is a fire, a world of iniquity.

It is an unruly evil, full of deadly poison. James iii, 6, 8.

A soft answer turneth away wrath; but grievous words stir up anger.

A wholesome tongue is a tree of life; but perverseness therein is a breach in the spirit. Proverbs xv, 1, 4.

Let all bitterness, and wrath, and anger, and clamor, and evil speaking, be put away from you, with all malice:

And be ye kind one to another, tender hearted, forgiving one another, as even God for Christ's sake hath forgiven you. Ephesians iv, 31, 32.

The Witch is yet at her work. She proceeded on her way, thankful that she has made one less shrew in the world.

CHAPTER VIII.

On her way along she observed a boy sitting on the walk near some shrubbery. He seemed very intent on whatever he was doing. She approached nearer and saw a poor butterfly denuded of its wings lying quivering in his hand, and he was looking at it with the most intense satisfaction.

"My lad, do you know that—

The eyes of the Lord are in every place, beholding the evil and the good. Proverbs xv, 3.

Even a child is known by his doings, whether his work be pure, and whether it be right. Proverbs xx, 11.

"Understand that it is sinful to torment any living thing."

The boy slunk away, realizing for the first time that it was wrong to torture anything so small as a butterfly.

The disposition to torture seems to be inherent with many boys and if allowed to grow on them will in time predominate over all good impulses, and prompt them to commit the most terrible crimes.

For the land is full of bloody crimes, and the city is full of violence. Ezekiel vii, 23.

If they were taught to cultivate will power to subdue these evil impulses what a blessing would be derived! How prone to wickedness is all human nature, and how much we need to pray for help to overcome it!

Watch and pray. Matthew xxvi, 41.

CHAPTER IX.

The Witch noticed a girl in the regulation uniform of white cap and apron marshalling several children. How oft seen in the want column: "A nurse girl who will wear the cap." Why was this headgear exacted as a badge of servitude? Why ape the Old World customs?

Say unto the king and to the queen, Humble yourselves, sit down; for your principalities shall come down, even the crown of your glory. Jeremiah xiii, 18.

Thus saith the Lord God: Remove the diadem and take off the crown; this shall not be the same; exalt him that is low, and abase him that is high.

I will overturn, overturn, overturn it; and it shall be no more until he come whose right it is; and I will give it him. Ezekiel xxi, 26, 27.

And the Lord alone shall be exalted in that day. Isaiah ii, 11.

Was not this government founded on the principle of equality? Did not the Pilgrim Fathers estimate one good as another if their righteousness was equal? And the distinction was made only between good and evil doers.

A nation that did righteousness, and forsook not the ordinance of their God. Isaiah lviii, 2.

And ye were now turned, and had done right in my sight in proclaiming liberty every man to his neighbor; and ye had made a covenant before me in the house which is called by my name:

But ye turned and polluted my name, and caused every man his servant, and every man his handmaid, whom he had set at liberty at their pleasure, to return, and brought them into subjection, to be unto you for servants and for handmaids. Jeremiah xxxiv, 16, 17.

Then, again, should it not be more essential for these mothers to look more after the morals of the persons who were to be companions for their children and to be less watchful of Mrs. Grundy's edicts?

For the customs of the people are vain.

They are altogether brutish and foolish; the stock is a doctrine of vanities.

They are vanity, and the work of errors; in the time of their visitation they shall perish. Jeremiah x, 3, 8, 15.

The Witch recalled an instance where a distinguished political leader married a sewing woman, and his bride was ostracized from society when it leaked out that she had labored for a livelihood. Had all these aristocrats as clean a record?

Am afraid one's hands would be somewhat soiled by too close investigation.

Ye are they which justify yourselves before men; but God knoweth your hearts. Luke xvi, 15.

For there is nothing covered that shall not be revealed; neither hid, that shall not be known. Luke xii, 2.

For God shall bring every work into judgment with every secret thing, whether it be good or whether it be evil. Ecclesiastes xii, 14.

The just Lord is in the midst thereof; he will not do iniquity; every morning doth he bring his judgment to light, he faileth not. Zephaniah iii, 5.

CHAPTER X.

One day when passing the jail our Witch was moved with an impulse to go inside. The warden allowed her to pass in. Her heart ached for these poor wretches whose faces from behind the bars looked so hopeless and unhappy, and whose blasphemous language chilled her. She longed for the time when:

Every one that nameth the name of Christ depart from iniquity. II Timothy ii, 19.

Who knew but these criminals were as innocent in the light of God's All-Searching Eye as those who less tried have committed less evil?

For all have sinned and come short of the glory of God. Romans iii, 23.

If we say that we have no sin we deceive ourselves, and the truth is not in us. John i, 8.

Some have better childhood memories of good influences brought to bear on their susceptible innocence, and would not humanity, begot and reared in iniquity, have a natural inclination to evil, and consequently be pardonable for greater crimes than those of a healthier nourishment? And would not those stronger ones with great mental gifts have more to answer for accordingly than those of weaker natures? Well, it is beyond any human comprehension to execute perfect justice.

Then hear thou from Heaven, thy dwelling place, and forgive, and render unto every man according unto all his ways, whose heart thou knowest; for thou only knowest the hearts of the children of men. II Chronicles vi, 30.

I, the Lord, search the heart, I try the reins, even to give every man according to his ways, and according to the fruit of his doings. Jeremiah xvii, 10.

The judgments of the Lord are true and righteous altogether. Psalms xix, 9.

But why dost thou judge thy brother? Or why doth thou set at nought thy brother? For we shall all stand before the judgment seat of Christ. Let us not therefore judge one another any more; but judge this rather, that no man put a stumbling block or an occasion to fall in his brother's way. Romans xiv, 10, 13.

Thou art inexcusable, O man, whosoever thou art, that judgest; for wherein thou judgest another, thou condemnest thyself. Romans ii, 1.

Judge not, and ye shall not be judged; condemn not, and ye shall not be condemned; forgive, and ye shall be forgiven. Luke vi, 37.

Therefore judge nothing before the time until the Lord come, who both will bring to light the hidden things of darkness, and will make manifest the counsels of the hearts. I Corinthians iv, 5.

But crime will come to an end in that happy time when we will know each other's innermost thoughts.

What a grand and awful time will be the day of judgment, when the Spirit quickens the dust of centuries! Grand for those who have sincerely tried to serve the King!

Who among us shall dwell with everlasting burnings? He that walketh righteously, and speaketh uprightly; he that despiseth the gain of oppressions, that shaketh his hands from holding of bribes, that stoppeth his ears from hearing of blood, and shutteth his eyes from seeing evil: he shall dwell on high; his place of defence shall be the munitions of rocks; bread shall be sure. Isaiah xxxiii, 14, 15, 16.

Blessed are they that keep his testimonies, and that seek him with the whole heart. Psalms cxix, 2.

They that feared the Lord spake often one to another; and the Lord hearkened and heard it, and a book of remembrance was written before him for them that feared the Lord, and that thought upon his name.

And they shall be mine, saith the Lord of Hosts, in that day when I make up my jewels; and I will spare them as a man spareth his own son that serveth him. Malachi iii, 16, 17.

Awful for the hypocrites when God's magnetic eyes burn into their souls. In this way the world of sin will be dissolved, but space, in which we move and have our being, will never be destroyed.

One generation passeth away and another generation cometh; but the earth abideth forever. Ecclesiastes i, 4.

For this hath the Lord said: The whole land shall be desolate, yet will I not make a full end. Jeremiah iv, 27.

Lift up your eyes to the heavens, and look upon the earth beneath; for the heavens shall vanish away like smoke, and the earth shall wax old like a garment, and they that dwell therein shall die in like manner; but my salvation shall be forever, and my righteousness shall not be abolished. Isaiah li, 6.

Who may abide the day of his coming? And who shall stand when he appeareth? For he is like a refiner's fire. Malachi iii, 2.

Every man's work shall be made manifest; for the day shall declare it, because it shall be revealed by fire; and the fire shall try every man's work of what sort it is. I Corinthians iii, 13.

For our God is a consuming fire. Hebrews xii, 29.

The earth and all the inhabitants thereof are dissolved; I bear up the pillars of it. Psalms lxxv, 3.

All the earth shall be devoured with the fire of my jealousy. Zephaniah iii, 8.

Their flesh shall consume away while they stand upon their feet, and their eyes shall consume away in their holes, and their tongue shall consume away in their mouth. Zechariah xiv, 12.

As wax melteth before the fire; so let the wicked perish at the presence of God. Psalms lxviii, 2.

Therefore the inhabitants of the earth are burned and few men left. Isaiah xxiv, 6.

All the hosts of heaven shall be dissolved, and the heavens shall be rolled together as a scroll. Isaiah xxxiv, 4.

Woe unto you, scribes and pharisees, hypocrites! for ye devour widow's houses, and for a pretense make long prayers. Therefore ye shall receive the greater damnation. Matthew xxiii, 14.

For the congregation of hypocrites shall be desolate, and fire shall consume the tabernacles of bribery. Job xv, 34.

I will bring you into the wilderness of the people, and there will I plead with you face to face.

And there shall ye remember your ways, and all your doings, wherein ye have been defiled; and ye shall loathe yourselves in your own sight for all your evils that ye have committed. Ezekiel xx, 35, 43.

CHAPTER XI.

The Witch was not a regular attendant at any house of worship of any set creed, but preferred ones of lesser grandeur, feeling that she met with more sincerity within. But one Sabbath morning her steps led to one of the largest and most fashionable churches in the city. The ushers were busy seating the well-dressed throng. She slipped along and took a seat by the side of a sumptuously dressed lady who shifted and spread her drapery a little more as a hint to the intruder that her presence was undesirable.

Many haughty glances of derision were shot at the poorly clad stranger who had presumed to come in their midst. She looked about her on the throng.

All is vanity. Ecclesiastes i, 2.

Richly attired matrons, conscious only of their extreme style; fair young girls, not a whit less extravagantly garbed than their elders, with cramped waists and all the accoutrements belonging to devotees of fashion.

A pity that such fair flowers like the rose could not remain longer in bud, for both fall into decay all too quickly after maturity. But Dame Fashion seems in a hurry and holds to artificial development.

Make not my Father's house a house of merchandise. John ii, 16.

What more was this great display of finery than one way of advertising goods?

Bring no more vain oblations; incense is an abomination unto me; the new moons and Sabbaths, the calling of assemblies, I cannot away with; it is iniquity, even the solemn meeting.

Wash you, make you clean; put away the evil of your doings from before mine eyes; cease to do evil.

Learn to do well; seek judgment, relieve the oppressed, judge the fatherless, plead for the widow.

Come now, and let us reason together, saith the Lord: though your sins be as scarlet they shall be as white as snow; though they be red like crimson, they shall be as wool.

If ye be willing and obedient, ye shall eat the good of the land.

But if ye refuse and rebel, ye shall be devoured. Isaiah i, 13, 16, 17, 18, 19, 20.

Their land also is full of idols; they worship the works of their own hands that which their own fingers have made. Isaiah ii, 8.

The daughters of Zion are haughty, and walk with stretched forth necks and wanton eyes, walking and mincing as they go, and making a tinkling with their feet.

In that day the Lord will take away the bravery of their tinkling ornaments about their feet, and their cauls, and their round tires like the moon.

The chains, and the bracelets, and the mufflers.

The bonnets, the headbands, and the earrings.

The rings.

The changeable suits of apparel, and the mantels, and the wimples, and the crisping pins.

The glasses, and the fine linen, and the hoods, and the veils. Isaiah iii, 16, 18, 19, 20, 21, 22, 23.

That women adorn themselves in modest apparel, with shamefacedness and sobriety; not with broidered hair, or gold, or pearls, or costly array;

But (which becometh women professing godliness) with good works. I Timothy ii, 9, 10.

The eloquent and eminent divine preached a flowery discourse with no reproof pointing to the vanity and frivolity of the hour.

They are shepherds that cannot understand; they all look to their own way, every one for his gain, from his quarter. Isaiah lvi, 11.

Many pastors have destroyed my vineyard; they have trodden my portion under foot. Jeremiah xii, 10.

The pastors are become brutish, and have not sought the Lord. Jeremiah x, 21.

Woe unto you, ye blind guides. Matthew xxiii, 16.

Whose mouths must be stopped, who subvert whole houses, teaching things which they ought not, for filthy lucre's sake. Titus i, 11.

Ye are departed out of the way; ye have caused many to stumble at the law. Malachi ii, 8.

Preach the word; be instant in season, out of season; reprove, rebuke, extort with all long suffering and doctrine.

For the time will come when they will not endure sound doctrine; but after their own lusts shall they heap to themselves teachers having itching ears;

And they shall turn away their ears from the truth, and shall be turned into fables.

But watch thou in all things, endure afflictions, do the work of an evangelist, make full proof of thy ministry. II Timothy iv, 2, 3, 4, 5.

The great organ reverberated through the building. The choir sang of God's love to all creatures alike. Two women sat side by side, and the one of loftier mien bowed her head, and for the first time in her life felt the love of God in her heart;

and the Witch went out from church happy, knowing that through her influence one soul was redeemed this Sabbath morning.

CHAPTER XII.

Marching along the road came the Salvation Army. A crowd of juveniles bent on hilarity followed in line, mimicking and ridiculing them. The crowd on the sidewalk jeered, and a high dignitary in church affairs joined his voice with the rest, remarking that this rabble never ought to be allowed to parade the streets Sunday. Who knows how many degraded lives have been elevated by this much ridiculed religious body who do good work in the slums where religion is most needful, and in so doing follow more closely in the footsteps of the Christ than those who spend their energy in striving among themselves for precedence in the public schools and everywhere?

Why all this contention? Should not real Christian worshippers work in harmony?

Have we not all one Father? Hath not one God created us? Malachi ii, 10.

And there was also a strife among them which of them should be accounted the greatest.

But ye shall not be so; but he that is greatest among you, let him be as the younger; and he that is chief, as he that doth serve. Luke xxii, 24, 26.

Do all things without murmurings and disputings. Philippians ii, 14.

Shun profane and vain babblings. II Timothy ii, 16.

Be at peace among yourselves. I Thessalonians v, 13.

Seek peace and pursue it. Psalms xxxiv, 14.

Let nothing be done through strife or vain glory. Philippians ii, 3.

Now the end of the commandment is charity out of a pure heart, and of a good conscience, and of faith unfeigned.

From which some having swerved have turned aside into vain jangling. I Timothy i, 5, 6.

Examine yourselves whether ye be in the faith; prove your own selves.

Be of one mind, live in peace. II Corinthians xiii, 5, 11.

Avoid foolish questions, and genealogies, and contentions, and strivings about the law; for they are unprofitable and vain. Titus iii, 9.

For where envying and strife is, there is confusion and every evil work. James iii, 16.

Now I beseech you brethren by the name of the Lord Jesus Christ, that ye all speak the same thing, and that there be no division among you; but that ye be perfectly joined together in the same mind and in the same judgment. I Corinthians i, 10.

I will therefore that men pray everywhere, lifting up holy hands, without wrath and doubting. I Timothy ii, 8.

Behold, ye fast for strife and debate.

Is not this the fast that I have chosen? to loose the bands of wickedness, to undo the heavy burdens, and to let the oppressed go free, and that ye brake every yoke?

Is it not to deal thy bread to the hungry, and that thou bring the poor that are cast out to thy house?

When thou seest the naked that thou cover him; and that thou hide not thyself from thine own flesh?

Then shall thy light break forth as the morning; and thy righteousness shall go before thee; the glory of the Lord shall be thy reward.

Then shalt thou call, and the Lord shall answer; thou shalt cry, and he shall say: Here I am. If thou take away from the midst of thee the yoke, the putting forth of the finger, and speaking vanity;

And if thou draw out thy soul to the hungry and satisfy the afflicted soul; then shall thy light rise in obscurity, and thy darkness be as noonday;

And the Lord shall guide thee continually. Isaiah lviii, 4, 6, 7, 8, 9, 10, 11.

Let us hear the conclusion of the whole matter: Fear God and keep his commandments, for this is the whole duty of man. Ecclesiastes xii, 13.

He hath showed thee, O Man, what is good; and what doth the Lord require of thee but to do justly, and to love mercy, and to walk humbly with thy God? Micah vi, 8.

CHAPTER XIII.

The Witch resumed work Monday morning. There was more stir in the streets than usual. On every corner were groups of excited men. Nothing but whisky and election would cause so much commotion.

The carriages of the different candidates were out scouring the town for voters.

Some of these aspirants for office had almost impoverished themselves by daily treating the crowd of loafers who are always ready to trade their votes for whisky.

They go about electioneering for themselves. Bosh! if a man has the elements of greatness he will find his place without all this self-praise.

For men to search their own glory is not glory. Proverbs xxv, 27.

For if a man think himself to be something, when he is nothing, he deceiveth himself. Galatians vi, 3.

Election day and no mistaking it; the saloons are supposed to be closed, but there is a back door to some of them.

It is not for kings to drink wine; nor for princes strong drink: Lest they drink and forget the law and pervert the judgment of any of the afflicted. Proverbs xxxi, 4, 5.

Is it any wonder that the women of our land clamor for a voice in the affairs of state and nation?

But a woman's place is not at the polls. She can do more good at home in training the minds of her sons, the future voters, and in making her husband's home-coming pleasant, that he may prefer it to haunts of vice. And it is to be hoped that man through debauchery will not become altogether inefficient and make it necessary for woman to take the lead.

But I suffer not a woman to teach nor to usurp authority over the man, but to be in silence. I Timothy ii, 12.

CHAPTER XIV.

In the evening at that most entrancing hour between daylight and dark, when all creation seems in a dreamy mood, the Witch found herself at the entrance of a gilded palace of sin. A number of the inmates were flitting about the flower-laden, well-kept grounds. She approached one of exquisite beauty of person whose face was not yet passion-scarred.

She was dressed in some soft, flowing, white material which gave her more of a seraphic appearance than one of sensualism. The Witch asked what brought her to this stage of immorality. The woman's reply was that she had been reared in wealth, but her father through some unlucky speculation lost everything. She had never learned to work, but had been taught that any labor was most degrading, and she had not qualified herself to teach any branch of learning, never having made allowance for the swift wings of vanishing wealth.

When thrown on her own resources she was at a loss to know what to do, when a wealthy gentleman friend came to her assistance at the sacrifice of her honor.

He soon tired of her, however; her father had died broken-hearted, and her mother was staying with a distant relative who had kindly offered her a home.

The Witch persuaded her to leave this life of disgrace, to learn honest work and brighten her mother's remaining years.

Study to show thyself approved unto God, a workman that needeth not to be ashamed. II Timothy ii, 15.

She said that it would be hard for her to face the world with this stigma of shame on her character; that all those bearing any claim to respectability would scorn her.

The Witch told her that God was judge and not the people, and their lives were not altogether blameless.

God is the judge. Psalms lxxv, 7.

He that is without sin among you, let him first cast a stone at her. John viii, 7.

The woman was undecided, but the better mind prevailed and she accompanied the Witch home, and the next day found respectable employment.

And still the good work goes on.

Reader, I am only narrating a small portion of this woman's work which she found as the days went by to be illimitable. *Vice versa.* If one possessing this mysterious power was inclined to evil rather than good, what a great amount of wickedness might be accomplished through it. God only knows how much of the good and evil that has been done in the world may be attributed to this hidden force.

Was the famed enchantress of the Nile gifted with this secret to a very great extent, and many other characters of history celebrated in their day for the influence they exercised?

CHAPTER XV.

The Witch heard of a murder trial that was going on in court and arousing intense interest, owing to the high social standing of all the parties concerned. She acted on impulse to a certain extent and, leaving her birds at home, started at once for the court-house.

On her way there she turned her attention to a case of street pugilism. A crowd of boys, ranging in age from seven to twenty, had congregated. Two small urchins were fighting; their faces were scratched and bleeding, and the crowd was urging them on to do each other more injury.

These young ruffians made a study of wickedness which is more than mischief, and this element is on an increase the world over.

Yea also the heart of the sons of men is full of evil. Ecclesiastes ix, 3.

No wonder when they have for examples men in high places who take such interest in prize fighting.

It would be more in keeping with their positions if their minds could aspire to something more elevating. They are ready enough to censure the Spaniards for their bull fights, but are themselves not far in advance when they will encourage this barbarous sport which seems to be gaining popularity.

The wicked walk on every side when the vilest men are exalted. Psalms xii, 8.

For the leaders of this people cause them to err; and they that are led of them are destroyed. Isaiah ix, 16.

These are the men that devise mischief and give wicked counsel in this city. Ezekiel xi, 2.

If they would exercise the spiritual nature more and the animal less they could take no pleasure in such brutish doing.

For the flesh lusteth against the Spirit, and the Spirit against the flesh; and these are contrary the one to the other. Galatians v, 17.

Even the Press takes a hand in it, and devotes whole columns of the papers to explaining in minutest detail the movements of the combatants.

Our Witch was wrapped in thought, but did not forget her work, and in a few moments after she appeared among them the shamefaced crowd dispersed.

CHAPTER XVI.

When the chief witness against the accused was called to give his testimony there was one among the throng of spectators whose eyes never left his face.

He started in a resolute manner, then wavered a little, and finally broke down in the midst of it and confessed his own guilt. He was the murderer.

Thou shalt not bear false witness against thy neighbor. Exodus xx, 16.

Confess your faults one to another, and pray one for another. James v, 16.

He that covereth his sins shall not prosper; but whoso confesseth and forsaketh them shall have mercy. Proverbs xxviii, 13.

If we confess our sins he is faithful and just to forgive us our sins, and to cleanse us from all unrighteousness. John i, 9.

There was a hush like the hush of death in the courtroom while he was speaking. When the crowd passed out, a plainly garbed figure went out also unobserved. The Witch had done her work for the day.

CHAPTER XVII.

She looked on the cars gliding over the electric road. What of this occult power? And what of her own? Eventually would electricity impel the entire universe?

Had this always existed and was yet to be brought out by masterful minds? Was this the connecting link between God and man? Then it was wisely said in ages past:

How long, ye simple ones, will ye love simplicity? Proverbs i, 22.

The Lord possessed me in the beginning of his way before his works of old.

When he prepared the heavens I was there; when he set a compass upon the face of the depth. Proverbs vii, 22, 27.

He ruleth by his power forever. Psalms lxvi, 7.

In the Lord Jehovah is everlasting strength. Isaiah xxvi, 4.

Take hold of my strength. Isaiah xxvii, 5.

Have ye not known? have ye not heard? hath it not been told you from the beginning? have ye not understood from the foundation of the earth? Isaiah xl, 21, 22.

For my people is foolish; they have not known me; they are sottish children, and they have none understanding; they are wise to do evil, but to do good they have no knowledge. Jeremiah iv, 22.

Understand, ye brutish among the people, and ye fools, when will ye be wise? Psalms xciv, 8.

O ye simple, understand wisdom; and ye fools, be ye of an understanding heart. Proverbs viii, 5.

Yea, if thou criest after knowledge, and liftest up thy voice for understanding;

If thou seekest her as silver, and searchest for her as for hid treasures;

Then shalt thou understand the fear of the Lord, and find the knowledge of God. Proverbs ii, 3, 4, 5.

He hath made the earth by his power, he hath established the world by his wisdom, and hath stretched out the heavens by his discretion.

When he uttereth his voice, there is a multitude of waters in the heavens, and he causeth the vapors to ascend from the ends of the earth; he maketh lightnings with rain, and bringeth forth the wind out of his treasures. Jeremiah x, 12, 13.

The heavens declare the glory of God; and the firmament sheweth his handiwork.

Day unto day uttereth speech, and night unto night sheweth knowledge.

There is no speech nor language where their voice is not heard.

Their line is gone out through all the earth, and their words to the end of the world. In them hath he set a tabernacle for the sun,

Which is as a bridegroom coming out of his chamber, and rejoiceth as a strong man to run a race.

His going forth is from the ends of the heaven, and his circuit unto the ends of it, and there is nothing hid from the heat thereof. Psalms xix, 1, 2, 3, 4, 5, 6.

The voice of the Lord is upon the waters; the God of glory thundereth, the Lord is upon many waters.

The voice of the Lord is powerful. Psalms xxix, 3, 4.

The thunder of his power who can understand? Job xxvi, 14.

With thee is the fountain of life; in thy light shall we see light. Psalms xxxvi, 9.

The earth shall be filled with the knowledge of the glory of the Lord, as the waters cover the sea. Habakkuk ii, 14.

Who is wise, and will observe these things, even they shall understand. Psalms cvii, 43.

At the resurrection, when the Lamb of God will rule the world as the center of gravitation like the sun, who among us can study mischief in secret when mind meets mind in one common thoroughfare of thought which cannot be divided by land or sea?

As the lightning cometh out of the east, and shineth even unto the west; so shall also the coming of the Son of Man be. Matthew xxiv, 27.

And the city hath no creed of the sun, neither of the moon, to shine in it; for the glory of God did lighten it, and the Lamb is the light thereof. Revelation xxi, 23.

The sun shall be no more thy light by day; neither for brightness shall the moon give light unto thee; but the Lord shall be unto thee an everlasting light, and thy God thy glory.

Thy sun shall no more go down; neither shall thy moon withdraw itself; for the Lord shall be thine everlasting light. Isaiah lx, 19, 20.

There shall be a resurrection of the dead, both of the just and unjust. Acts xxiv, 15.

As the Father raiseth up the dead and quickeneth them, even so the Son quickeneth whom he will. John v, 21.

Ye shall know that I am the Lord, when I have opened your graves, O my people, and brought you up out of your graves.

And shall put my spirit in you, and ye shall live. Ezekiel xxxvii, 13, 14.

The dead men shall live together; with my dead body shall they arise.

Awake and sing, ye that dwell in dust; for thy dew is as the dew of herbs, and the earth shall cast out the dead. Isaiah xxvi, 19.

CHAPTER XVIII.

One morning when near a handsome residence the Witch stopped at the sound of a musical instrument. The music ceased and a lady of forty or thereabout answered her ring.

She was surrounded with every luxury, but our Witch soon learned that here, too, was trouble. Yes, another mismated couple.

The lady said that her husband and herself had never lived very happily together after the first few months of married life; and recently another woman had come between them, and her husband, desirous of a separation, was about to commence proceedings for a divorce from her. As for herself it mattered little, but for the sake of her children she had rather it would not be.

Presently the husband came. He was a fine-looking man of pleasing address and unless appearance was deceiving he would do very well if started on the right track.

Here was more work for the ever busy brain.

Lo, this only have I found, that God hath made man upright; but they have sought out many inventions. Ecclesiastes vii, 29.

Yet I had planted thee a noble vine, wholly a right seed; how then art thou turned into the degenerate plant of a strange vine unto me? Jeremiah ii, 21.

He sat down facing the Witch, and after a little time was conscious of a new train of thoughts. His better spirit moved. Would it not be as well to live the remainder of his life with the mother of his children whom he dearly loved?

What therefore God hath joined together let not man put asunder. Matthew xix, 6.

Contract marriage is most suitable for the present age. That leaves the contracting parties on a grade with the cattle and admits of their changing companions whenever and as often as they like without breaking God's holy vows.

And this have ye done again, covering the altar of the Lord with tears, with weeping, and with crying out, insomuch that he regardeth not the offering any more, or receive it with good will at your hand.

Because the Lord hath been witness between thee and the wife of thy youth, against whom thou hast dealt treacherously; yet is she thy companion and the wife of thy covenant.

And did not he make one? yet had he the residue of the spirit.

Therefore take heed to your spirit, and let none deal treacherously against the wife of his youth.

For the Lord, the God of Israel, saith that he hateth putting away. Malachi ii, 13, 14, 15, 16.

If a man put away his wife and she go from him, and become another man's, shall not that land be greatly polluted? Jeremiah iii, 1.

When a marriage is solemnized by the word of God, then no law on earth is justifiable for breaking it; and when a couple truly love each other what but death can separate them? For misfortune of any kind only binds the tie of sympathy more closely.

If this tie was not so easily broken more persons would consider whom they were marrying and what they were marrying for, and if less deception was practiced beforehand, there would be fewer marriages which prove such dismal failures.

The heart is deceitful above all things, and desperately wicked; who can know it? Jeremiah xvii, 9.

We will be done with all this in the resurrection.

In the resurrection they neither marry, nor are given in marriage, but are as the angels of God in heaven. Matthew xxii, 30.

When the Witch left this pair she was happy in the thought that they would live together on better terms, and be like a re-united family.

CHAPTER XIX.

Later in the day our Witch was in another part of the city; while walking through an alley, she saw a Chinaman carrying a large basket full of clean clothes that he was returning to the owners. The Witch also noticed several half-grown boys and heard one of them remark:

"Say we take a shot at that heathen."

So with one accord they commenced pelting him with everything available. Their victim tried to defend himself to the best of his ability, but the half dozen boys pounced on him, and in the fracas the clothes were upset into the street.

It was hard to tell how far they would carry their vicious work, which they considered a capital joke, when some one appeared among them who was also at work. Very soon they all left off, not knowing why. The Witch stood near while he gathered up the clothes, which necessarily must be washed over again.

Then she tried to solve in her mind this Chinese problem:

These Mongolians are in a measure obnoxious, but as a rule are peaceable and industrious, which is more than can be said of many other people.

They have few opportunities for making a living in their own over-populous country, but perhaps when they have become more thoroughly Christianized, the race will be less prolific, which would be beneficial to their own nation and others.

Say among the heathen that the Lord reigneth. Psalms xcvi, 10.

For the more a man leans to divinity the less he cleaves to his animal nature; and what is true of the Chinese applies to other densely populated countries.

For they that are after the flesh do mind the things of the flesh; but they that are after the Spirit, the things of the Spirit. Romans viii, 5.

Let not sin therefore reign in your mortal body, that ye should obey it in the lusts thereof. Romans vi, 12.

For all that is in the world, the lust of the flesh, and the lust of the eyes, and the pride of life, is not of the Father, but is of the world.

And the world passeth away, and the lust thereof; but he that doeth the will of God abideth forever. John ii, 16, 17.

Her mind reverted to an incident which she witnessed in a cemetery. It was the Sabbath and she was walking about in there as she often did on this day, for what more forcible sermon can be delivered than a thinking mind can feel while moving about among the dead?

After a time she was conscious of a disturbance of some kind going on at one corner of the enclosure. A promiscuous crowd had gathered and ere long there came a Chinese funeral train and stopped at the open grave.

Then the crowd mocked them, and by this time it was evident that they had gathered there to have sport at the expense of the mourners.

The children were cutting up all manner of antics, and the parents stood by highly amused at the proceedings. It was almost impossible to conduct the burial rites on account of the confusion made by the mob.

To be sure it was a peculiar ceremony, but some respect ought to have been due the feelings of these sorrowing ones at such a time. These children were wholly undisciplined in the matter of right and wrong; their behavior was like so many young savages.

What were their parents teaching them? To selfishly enjoy the discomfort of others, and this was all, never trying to encourage the finer and better feelings in their natures.

Our Witch did not wait till the ceremony was over. Thoroughly disgusted with human nature, she left the cemetery.

CHAPTER XX.

She thought still less of it that night when awakened from sleep by a gang of boisterous picnickers who, full of liquor, were returning home from a day of revelry. Women's and men's voices mingled together in singing vile songs.

How wholly depraved are some natures, and how necessary that these lewd minds should be purified by a closer communion with more spiritual intellects!

When there are seven days in a week and our King only exacts from us the Sabbath it does seem as if He is entitled to that, but where people are confined to employment every day in the week but one, it is hardly probable that the kind Father would object to their having an outing on their one day of liberty out of a week of unremitting toil, if they would conduct themselves properly.

Not in rioting and drunkenness; not in chambering and wantonness. But put ye on the Lord Jesus Christ, and make not provision for the flesh to fulfill the lusts thereof. Romans xiii, 13, 14.

My Sabbaths they greatly polluted.

I am the Lord your God; walk in my statutes, and hallow my Sabbaths. Ezekiel xx, 13.

Thus saith the Lord, keep ye judgment, and do justice.

Blessed is the man that doeth this, and the son of man that layeth hold on it; that keepeth the Sabbath from polluting it, and keepeth his hand from doing any evil. Isaiah lvi, 1, 2.

If thou turn away thy foot from the Sabbath, from doing thy pleasure on my holy day; and call the Sabbath a delight, the holy of the Lord, honorable; and shalt honour him, not doing thine own ways, nor finding thine own pleasure, nor speaking thine own words:

Then shalt thou delight thyself in the Lord; and I will cause thee to ride upon the high places of the earth, and feed thee with the heritage of Jacob thy father; for the mouth of the Lord hath spoken it. Isaiah lviii, 13, 14.

But ere long a few cannot monopolize all the comforts, nor the masses be obliged to struggle hard every hour for the bare necessities of life, for who can defraud his neighbor when all minds will be a unit? and if honesty was practiced to the letter, the good things of life would not be so unequally divided.

The profit of the earth is for all. Ecclesiastes v, 9.

Yet ye say, the way of the Lord is not equal. Is not my way equal? Are not your ways unequal? Ezekiel xviii, 25.

For every one from the least even unto the greatest is given to covetousness, from the prophet even unto the priest, every one dealeth falsely. Jeremiah viii, 10.

Their tongue is an arrow shot out; it speaketh deceit; one speaketh peaceably to his neighbor with his mouth, but in heart he layeth wait. Jeremiah ix, 8.

As a cage is full of birds, so are their houses full of deceit; therefore they are become great, and waxen rich. Jeremiah v, 27.

Behold these are the ungodly who prosper in the world; they increase in riches. Psalms lxxiii, 12.

Thus saith the Lord, execute ye judgment and righteousness, and deliver the spoiled out of the hand of the oppressor; and do no wrong, do no violence to the stranger, the fatherless, nor the widow. Jeremiah xxii, 3.

Be renewed in the spirit of your mind; putting away lying, speak every man truth with his neighbor; for we are members one of another. Ephesians iv, 23, 25.

That they all may be one; as thou, Father, art in me, and I in thee, that they also may be one in us. John xvii, 21.

Behold, how good and how pleasant it is for brethren to dwell together in unity! Psalms cxxxiii, 1.

CHAPTER XXI.

Ever on the alert to do good the Witch stopped at a rickety tenement, with nothing to recommend it but a climbing rose-bush, set out by some flower-loving tenant a number of years before, and which twined its long branches in full bloom over one end of the dilapidated structure; it was an illustration of extremes meeting, this perfectly beautiful rose-bush and the unsightly old porch. The landlady did not care to buy a bird, and none of the occupants of her rooms were at home during the day, except one, who poor boy, was always in, and a visitor would be sure to cheer him up a bit, though it would be useless to try and sell a bird there. She led the way up a flight of stairs to the room where a little cripple was amusing himself with a few marbles that he was rolling about on the table by which he was sitting.

He was delighted with the birds, but knew that his sister could not afford to buy him one. He said she was employed up town in a store, naming the business block of a well-known and very wealthy merchant, and he could not go out and play like other boys, and the days seemed very long sometimes.

Yes, thought our Witch, a day must be a long time to this poor weakling with little to amuse him.

She gave him his choice of the birds, and after promising to bring it back in the evening with a new cage which she would buy for him, the Witch took her leave.

CHAPTER XXII.

A little way down the street in advance of her was a heavy wagon drawn by one patient horse that looked as though it might have seen better days, but now one could numerate every rib in its worn frame.

The driver was beating the poor animal unmercifully. It doubtless had a history, and if allowed speech would tell of a gradual decline, of careful nourishment and little to do in its prime, but when strength and beauty began to wane, of a harder life, and now in old age when attention was most needful, must fall in line with the great majority of overworked, under-fed beasts of burden, and some day when no longer able to hold up the harness, would be taken out and shot.

Our Witch could hear in her mind's ear the rebuke of old:

What have I done unto thee, that thou has smitten me these three times? Numbers xxii, 28.

She watched the man intently for a few seconds, and then his arm dropped to his side. Why this sudden sympathy so foreign to his hardened nature?

The All-seeing Eye must often look down in tenderest pity on this ill-treated animal creation, which is more deserving of His regard than these inhuman beings, who by their cruelty place themselves far below a level with the lower animals.

The Lord is good to all; and His tender mercies are over all His works. Psalms cxlv, 9.

Be ye therefore merciful, as your Father is also merciful. Luke vi, 36.

The merciful man doeth good to his own soul: but he that is cruel troubleth his own flesh. Proverbs xi, 17.

Surely the Society for the Prevention of Cruelty to Animals is one of the noblest organizations of modern times, and for good work stands second to no religious denomination that has ever existed, or ever will exist.

CHAPTER XXIII.

Her next stopping place was not in a rookery part of the city, but was where wealth abounds. It was just before the noon hour when she entered the palatial home of a many times millionaire and was ushered into the library where he was busy with some papers. "Would you care to buy a bird, sir?"

"I have no time to talk with you this morning, madam." He looked at her uneasily, and mentally resolved to administer a reproof to the servant for allowing these tramping peddlers to enter the house.

The magnetic power was again brought into requisition.

The Witch might have used this influence for her own financial advantage, but was too conscientious for that, and furthermore money was not her aim in life.

Gradually there came stealing into this rich man's brain new thoughts; was he doing right with his boundless wealth? He could not understand why he was just waking up to the fact that he had not.

How many needy ones had he passed by?

Withhold not good to them to whom it is due, when it is in the power of thine hand to do it. Proverbs iii, 27.

To endow some charitable institution at his death, as a monument to his own memory, would hardly atone for neglected duty. Would God hold him responsible for this neglect and bar him from the Kingdom?

Thou art weighed in the balances, and art found wanting. Daniel v, 27.

Woe unto him that buildeth his house by unrighteousness, and his chambers by wrong; that useth his neighbor's service without wages, and giveth him not for his work. Thine eyes and thine heart are not but for thy covetousness. Jeremiah xxii, 13, 17.

Your riches are corrupted, and your garments are moth-eaten. Your gold and silver is cankered; and the rust of them shall be a witness against you and shall eat your flesh as it were fire. Ye have heaped treasures together for the last days. Behold the hire of the laborers who have reaped down your fields, which is of you kept back by fraud, crieth: and the cries of them which reaped are entered into the ears of the Lord of Sabaoth. James v, 2, 3, 4.

Who so stoppeth his ears at the cry of the poor, he shall cry himself, but shall not be heard. Proverbs xxi, 13.

Let not the rich man glory in his riches. Jeremiah ix, 23.

Neither their silver nor their gold shall be able to deliver them in the day of the Lord's wrath. Zephaniah i, 18.

Charge them that are rich in this world, that they be not high-minded, nor trust in uncertain riches, but in the living God, who giveth us richly all things to enjoy. That they do good, that they be rich in good works, ready to distribute. I Timothy vi, 17, 18.

He that oppresseth the poor reproacheth his Maker: but he that honoreth Him hath mercy on the poor. Proverbs xiv, 31.

As a partridge sitteth on eggs, and hatcheth them not; so he that getteth riches, and not by right, shall leave them in the midst of his days, and at his end shall be a fool. Jeremiah xvii, 11.

CHAPTER XXIV.

Faithful to her promise, the Witch purchased a cage, and early in the evening returned to the cripple's abode and was joyfully greeted.

"O, but you are a good lady to think of me, only a cripple boy!"

She felt that it was indeed more blessed to give than to receive (Acts XX, 35) when one could do God a service at the same time.

As ye have done it unto the least of these ye have done it unto Me. Matthew xxv, 40.

He that hath pity upon the poor lendeth to the Lord. Proverbs xix, 17.

In a short time the sister came. His face brightened up with pleasure when he told her of the present he had received; now he would have a companion all through the long days.

She was also in a happy mood. The head of the firm where she worked had raised the salary of all his employes, and she was very thankful for her good luck because of her brother who needed more books and toys, for the poor child had to amuse himself the best he could during the day. The Witch returned home. She saw the progress of her work many times after in this millionaire's acts of benevolence which were so liberal as to excite press comment.

Blessed is he that considereth the poor; the Lord will deliver him in time of trouble. Psalms xli, 1.

CHAPTER XXV.

Our Witch read of the doings in the old world and was sorry that distance and sea prevented this influence from being brought to bear upon some of the crowned heads, who, born to almost absolute power, showed no mercy to a religious sect, who according to Holy Writ are the chosen people of God. But one alone cannot revolutionize the earth, unless that one be omnipotent.

Some day this persecution must come to an end.

For the Lord will have mercy on Jacob, and will yet choose Israel, and set them in their own land, and the stranger shall be joined with them. Isaiah xiv, 1.

Prepare to meet thy God, O Israel. Amos iv, 12.

The great day of the Lord is near, it is near, and hasteth greatly. Zephaniah i, 14.

Let all the inhabitants of the land tremble, for the day of the Lord cometh, for it is nigh at hand. Joel, ii, 1.

But of that day and hour no man, no not the angels of heaven, but my Father only. Watch, therefore, for ye know not what hour your Lord doth come. Matthew xxiv, 36, 42.

Obey, I beseech thee, the voice of the Lord, which I speak unto thee, so it shall be well unto thee, and thy soul shall live. Jeremiah xxxviii, 20.

Return ye now every one from his evil way and make your ways and your doings good. Jeremiah xviii, 11.

And to wait for his Son from heaven whom he raised from the dead, even Jesus, which delivered us from the wrath to come. 1 Thessalonians i, 10.

Neither is there salvation in any other; for there is none other name under heaven given among men, whereby we must be saved. Acts iv, 12.

There is therefore now no condemnation to them which are in Christ Jesus who walk not after the flesh, but after the Spirit. Romans viii, 1.

Draw nigh to God and he will draw nigh to you;

Cleanse your hands, ye sinners, and purify your hearts, ye double minded. James iv, 8.

Behold, I stand at the door and knock: if any man hear my voice, and open the door, I will come in to him, and will sup with him, and he with me. Revelation iii, 20.

I will heal their backsliding, I will love them freely. Hosea xiv, 4.

Repent ye, therefore, and be converted, that your sins may be blotted out when the times of refreshing shall come from the presence of the Lord; and he shall send Jesus Christ, which before was preached unto you. Acts iii, 19, 20.

If ye thoroughly amend your ways and your doings; if ye thoroughly execute judgment between a man and his neighbor;

If ye oppress not the stranger, the fatherless, and the widow, and shed not innocent blood in this place, neither walk after other gods to your hurt;

Then will I cause you to dwell in this place, in the land I gave to your fathers, for ever and ever. Obey my voice and I will be your God, and ye shall be my people. Jeremiah vii, 5, 6, 7, 23.

Therefore, turn thou to thy God; keep mercy and judgment, and wait on thy God continually. Hosea xii, 6.

Depart from evil and do good, and dwell for evermore. Psalms xxxvii, 27.

The redeemed of the Lord shall return, and come singing unto Zion; and everlasting joy shall be upon their head; they shall obtain gladness and joy; and sorrow and mourning shall flee away. Isaiah li, 11.

And it shall come to pass that he that is left in Zion, and he that remaineth in Jerusalem shall be called holy, even every one that is written among the living in Jerusalem. When the Lord shall have washed away the filth of the daughters of Zion, and shall have purged the blood of Jerusalem from the midst thereof by the spirit of judgment, and by the spirit of burning. Isaiah iv, 3, 4.

Behold, I come quickly. And the Spirit and the bride say, come; and let him that heareth say, come; and let him that is athirst come; and whosoever will, let him take the water of life freely. Revelation xxii, 7, 17.

CHAPTER XXVI.

The Witch did not go about her work the next day, nor the next, for somehow she contracted a severe cold which completely prostrated her, and then pneumonia clutched her throat.

One morning, when the first golden rays of the sun glanced over the sleeping city, they rested in benediction on her death bed. A neighbor, whom in time past she had befriended, was at her side.

She knew that the end was near.

Will this influence stop here? or will it go on and on through all the ages to come?

Blessed are the dead which die in the Lord from henceforth: Yea, saith the Spirit, that they may rest from their labours; and their works do follow them. Revelation xiv, 13.

The Witch

Anton Chekhov

THE WITCH

IT was approaching nightfall. The sexton, Savely Gykin, was lying in his huge bed in the hut adjoining the church. He was not asleep, though it was his habit to go to sleep at the same time as the hens. His coarse red hair peeped from under one end of the greasy patchwork quilt, made up of coloured rags, while his big unwashed feet stuck out from the other. He was listening. His hut adjoined the wall that encircled the church and the solitary window in it looked out upon the open country. And out there a regular battle was going on. It was hard to say who was being wiped off the face of the earth, and for the sake of whose destruction nature was being churned up into such a ferment; but, judging from the unceasing malignant roar, someone was getting it very hot. A victorious force was in full chase over the fields, storming in the forest and on the church roof, battering spitefully with its fists upon the windows, raging and tearing, while something vanquished was howling and wailing.... A plaintive lament sobbed at the window, on the roof, or in the stove. It sounded not like a call for help, but like a cry of misery, a consciousness that it was too late, that there was no salvation. The snowdrifts were covered with a thin coating of ice; tears quivered on them and on the trees; a dark slush of mud and melting snow flowed along the roads and paths. In short, it was thawing, but through the dark night the heavens failed to see it, and flung flakes of fresh snow upon the melting earth at a terrific rate. And the wind staggered like a drunkard. It would not let the snow settle on the ground, and whirled it round in the darkness at random.

Savely listened to all this din and frowned. The fact was that he knew, or at any rate suspected, what all this racket outside the window was tending to and whose handiwork it was.

"I know!" he muttered, shaking his finger menacingly under the bedclothes; "I know all about it."

On a stool by the window sat the sexton's wife, Raissa Nilovna. A tin lamp standing on another stool, as though timid and distrustful of its powers, shed a dim and flickering light on her broad shoulders, on the handsome, tempting-looking contours of her person, and on her thick plait, which reached to the floor. She was making sacks out of coarse hempen stuff. Her hands moved nimbly, while her whole body, her eyes, her eyebrows, her full lips, her white neck were as still as though they were asleep, absorbed in the monotonous, mechanical toil. Only from time to time she raised her head to rest her weary neck, glanced for a moment towards the window, beyond which the snowstorm was raging, and bent again over her sacking. No desire, no joy, no grief, nothing was expressed by her handsome face with its turned-up nose and its dimples. So a beautiful fountain expresses nothing when it is not playing.

But at last she had finished a sack. She flung it aside, and, stretching luxuriously, rested her motionless, lack-lustre eyes on the window. The panes were swimming with drops like tears, and white with short-lived snowflakes which fell on the window, glanced at Raissa, and melted....

"Come to bed!" growled the sexton. Raissa remained mute. But suddenly her eyelashes flickered and there was a gleam of attention in her eye. Savely, all the time watching her expression from under the quilt, put out his head and asked:

"What is it?"

"Nothing.... I fancy someone's coming," she answered quietly.

The sexton flung the quilt off with his arms and legs, knelt up in bed, and looked blankly at his wife. The timid light of the lamp illuminated his hirsute, pock-marked countenance and glided over his rough matted hair.

"Do you hear?" asked his wife.

Through the monotonous roar of the storm he caught a scarcely audible thin and jingling monotone like the shrill note of a gnat when it wants to settle on one's cheek and is angry at being prevented.

"It's the post," muttered Savely, squatting on his heels.

Two miles from the church ran the posting road. In windy weather, when the wind was blowing from the road to the church, the inmates of the hut caught the sound of bells.

"Lord! fancy people wanting to drive about in such weather," sighed Raissa.

"It's government work. You've to go whether you like or not."

The murmur hung in the air and died away.

"It has driven by," said Savely, getting into bed.

But before he had time to cover himself up with the bedclothes he heard a distinct sound of the bell. The sexton looked anxiously at his wife, leapt out of bed and walked, waddling, to and fro by the stove. The bell went on ringing for a little, then died away again as though it had ceased.

"I don't hear it," said the sexton, stopping and looking at his wife with his eyes screwed up.

But at that moment the wind rapped on the window and with it floated a shrill jingling note. Savely turned pale, cleared his throat, and flopped about the floor with his bare feet again.

"The postman is lost in the storm," he wheezed out glancing malignantly at his wife. "Do you hear? The postman has lost his way!... I... I know! Do you suppose I... don't understand?" he muttered. "I know all about it, curse you!"

"What do you know?" Raissa asked quietly, keeping her eyes fixed on the window.

"I know that it's all your doing, you she-devil! Your doing, damn you! This snowstorm and the post going wrong, you've done it all—you!"

"You're mad, you silly," his wife answered calmly.

"I've been watching you for a long time past and I've seen it. From the first day I married you I noticed that you'd bitch's blood in you!"

"Tfoo!" said Raissa, surprised, shrugging her shoulders and crossing herself. "Cross yourself, you fool!"

"A witch is a witch," Savely pronounced in a hollow, tearful voice, hurriedly blowing his nose on the hem of his shirt; "though you are my wife, though you are of a clerical family, I'd say what you are even at confession.... Why, God have mercy upon us! Last year on the Eve of the Prophet Daniel and the Three Young Men there was a snowstorm, and what happened then? The mechanic came in to warm himself. Then on St. Alexey's Day the ice broke on the river and the district policeman turned up, and he was chatting with you all night... the damned brute! And when he came out in the morning and I looked at him, he had rings under his eyes and his cheeks were hollow! Eh? During the August fast there were two storms and each time the huntsman turned up. I saw it all, damn him! Oh, she is redder than a crab now, aha!"

"You didn't see anything."

"Didn't I! And this winter before Christmas on the Day of the Ten Martyrs of Crete, when the storm lasted for a whole day and night—do you remember?—the marshal's clerk was lost, and turned up here, the hound.... Tfoo! To be tempted by the clerk! It was worth upsetting God's weather for him! A drivelling scribbler, not a foot from the ground, pimples all over his mug and his neck awry! If he were good-looking, anyway—but he, tfoo! he is as ugly as Satan!"

The sexton took breath, wiped his lips and listened. The bell was not to be heard, but the wind banged on the roof, and again there came a tinkle in the darkness.

"And it's the same thing now!" Savely went on. "It's not for nothing the postman is lost! Blast my eyes if the postman isn't looking for you! Oh, the devil is a good hand at his work; he is a fine one to help! He will turn him round and round and bring him here. I know, I see! You can't conceal it, you devil's bauble, you heathen wanton! As soon as the storm began I knew what you were up to."

"Here's a fool!" smiled his wife. "Why, do you suppose, you thick-head, that I make the storm?"

"H'm!... Grin away! Whether it's your doing or not, I only know that when your blood's on fire there's sure to be bad weather, and when there's bad weather there's bound to be some crazy fellow turning up here. It happens so every time! So it must be you!"

To be more impressive the sexton put his finger to his forehead, closed his left eye, and said in a singsong voice:

"Oh, the madness! oh, the unclean Judas! If you really are a human being and not a witch, you ought to think what if he is not the mechanic, or the clerk, or the huntsman, but the devil in their form! Ah! You'd better think of that!"

"Why, you are stupid, Savely," said his wife, looking at him compassionately. "When father was alive and living here, all sorts of people used to come to him to be cured of the ague: from the village, and the hamlets, and the Armenian settlement. They came almost every day, and no one called them devils. But if anyone once a year comes in bad weather to warm himself, you wonder at it, you silly, and take all sorts of notions into your head at once."

His wife's logic touched Savely. He stood with his bare feet wide apart, bent his head, and pondered. He was not firmly convinced yet of the truth of his suspicions, and his wife's genuine and unconcerned tone quite disconcerted him. Yet after a moment's thought he wagged his head and said:

"It's not as though they were old men or bandy-legged cripples; it's always young men who want to come for the night.... Why is that? And if they only wanted to warm themselves——But they are up to mischief. No, woman; there's no creature in this world as cunning as your female sort! Of real brains you've not an ounce, less than a starling, but for devilish slyness—oo-oo-oo! The Queen of Heaven protect us! There is the postman's bell! When the storm was only beginning I knew all that was in your mind. That's your witchery, you spider!"

"Why do you keep on at me, you heathen?" His wife lost her patience at last. "Why do you keep sticking to it like pitch?"

"I stick to it because if anything—God forbid—happens to-night... do you hear?... if anything happens to-night, I'll go straight off to-morrow morning to Father Nikodim and tell him all about it. 'Father Nikodim,' I shall say, 'graciously excuse me, but she is a witch.' 'Why so?' 'H'm! do you want to know why?' 'Certainly....' And I shall tell him. And woe to you, woman! Not only at the dread Seat of Judgment, but in your earthly life you'll be punished, too! It's not for nothing there are prayers in the breviary against your kind!"

Suddenly there was a knock at the window, so loud and unusual that Savely turned pale and almost dropped backwards with fright. His wife jumped up, and she, too, turned pale.

"For God's sake, let us come in and get warm!" they heard in a trembling deep bass. "Who lives here? For mercy's sake! We've lost our way."

"Who are you?" asked Raissa, afraid to look at the window.

"The post," answered a second voice.

"You've succeeded with your devil's tricks," said Savely with a wave of his hand. "No mistake; I am right! Well, you'd better look out!"

The sexton jumped on to the bed in two skips, stretched himself on the feather mattress, and sniffing angrily, turned with his face to the wall. Soon he felt a draught of cold air on his back. The door creaked and the tall figure of a man, plastered over with snow from head to foot, appeared in the doorway. Behind him could be seen a second figure as white.

"Am I to bring in the bags?" asked the second in a hoarse bass voice.

"You can't leave them there." Saying this, the first figure began untying his hood, but gave it up, and pulling it off impatiently with his cap, angrily flung it near the stove. Then taking off his greatcoat, he threw that down beside it, and, without saying good-evening, began pacing up and down the hut.

He was a fair-haired, young postman wearing a shabby uniform and black rusty-looking high boots. After warming himself by walking to and fro, he sat down at the table, stretched out his muddy feet towards the sacks and leaned his chin on his fist. His pale face, reddened in places by the cold, still bore vivid traces of the pain and terror he had just been through. Though distorted by anger and bearing traces of recent suffering, physical and moral, it was handsome in spite of the melting snow on the eyebrows, moustaches, and short beard.

"It's a dog's life!" muttered the postman, looking round the walls and seeming hardly able to believe that he was in the warmth. "We were nearly lost! If it had not been for your light, I don't know what would have happened. Goodness only knows when it will all be over! There's no end to this dog's life! Where have we come?" he asked, dropping his voice and raising his eyes to the sexton's wife.

"To the Gulyaevsky Hill on General Kalinovsky's estate," she answered, startled and blushing.

"Do you hear, Stepan?" The postman turned to the driver, who was wedged in the doorway with a huge mail-bag on his shoulders. "We've got to Gulyaevsky Hill."

"Yes... we're a long way out." Jerking out these words like a hoarse sigh, the driver went out and soon after returned with another bag, then went out once more and this time brought the postman's sword on a big belt, of the pattern of that long flat blade with which Judith is portrayed by the bedside of Holofernes in cheap woodcuts. Laying the bags along the wall, he went out into the outer room, sat down there and lighted his pipe.

"Perhaps you'd like some tea after your journey?" Raissa inquired.

"How can we sit drinking tea?" said the postman, frowning. "We must make haste and get warm, and then set off, or we shall be late for the mail train. We'll stay ten minutes and then get on our way. Only be so good as to show us the way."

"What an infliction it is, this weather!" sighed Raissa.

"H'm, yes.... Who may you be?"

"We? We live here, by the church.... We belong to the clergy.... There lies my husband. Savely, get up and say good-evening! This used to be a separate parish till eighteen months ago. Of course, when the gentry lived here there were more people, and it was worth while to have the services. But now the gentry have gone, and I need not tell you there's nothing for the clergy to live on. The nearest village is Markovka, and that's over three miles away. Savely is on the retired list now, and has got the watchman's job; he has to look after the church...."

And the postman was immediately informed that if Savely were to go to the General's lady and ask her for a letter to the bishop, he would be given a good berth. "But he doesn't go to the General's lady because he is lazy and afraid of people. We belong to the clergy all the same..." added Raissa.

"What do you live on?" asked the postman.

"There's a kitchen garden and a meadow belonging to the church. Only we don't get much from that," sighed Raissa. "The old skinflint, Father Nikodim, from the next village celebrates here on St. Nicolas' Day in the winter and on St. Nicolas' Day in the summer, and for that he takes almost all the crops for himself. There's no one to stick up for us!"

"You are lying," Savely growled hoarsely. "Father Nikodim is a saintly soul, a luminary of the Church; and if he does take it, it's the regulation!"

"You've a cross one!" said the postman, with a grin. "Have you been married long?"

"It was three years ago the last Sunday before Lent. My father was sexton here in the old days, and when the time came for him to die, he went to the Consistory and asked them to send some unmarried man to marry me that I might keep the place. So I married him."

"Aha, so you killed two birds with one stone!" said the postman, looking at Savely's back. "Got wife and job together."

Savely wriggled his leg impatiently and moved closer to the wall. The postman moved away from the table, stretched, and sat down on the mail-bag. After a moment's thought he squeezed the bags with his hands, shifted his sword to the other side, and lay down with one foot touching the floor.

"It's a dog's life," he muttered, putting his hands behind his head and closing his eyes. "I wouldn't wish a wild Tatar such a life."

Soon everything was still. Nothing was audible except the sniffing of Savely and the slow, even breathing of the sleeping postman, who uttered a deep prolonged "h-h-h" at every breath. From time to time there was a sound like a creaking wheel in his throat, and his twitching foot rustled against the bag.

Savely fidgeted under the quilt and looked round slowly. His wife was sitting on the stool, and with her hands pressed against her cheeks was gazing at the postman's face. Her face was immovable, like the face of some one frightened and astonished.

"Well, what are you gaping at?" Savely whispered angrily.

"What is it to you? Lie down!" answered his wife without taking her eyes off the flaxen head.

Savely angrily puffed all the air out of his chest and turned abruptly to the wall. Three minutes later he turned over restlessly again, knelt up on the bed, and with his hands on the pillow looked askance at his wife. She was still sitting motionless, staring at the visitor. Her cheeks were pale and her eyes were glowing with a strange fire. The sexton cleared his throat, crawled on his stomach off the bed, and going up to the postman, put a handkerchief over his face.

"What's that for?" asked his wife.

"To keep the light out of his eyes."

"Then put out the light!"

Savely looked distrustfully at his wife, put out his lips towards the lamp, but at once thought better of it and clasped his hands.

"Isn't that devilish cunning?" he exclaimed. "Ah! Is there any creature slyer than womenkind?"

"Ah, you long-skirted devil!" hissed his wife, frowning with vexation. "You wait a bit!"

And settling herself more comfortably, she stared at the postman again.

It did not matter to her that his face was covered. She was not so much interested in his face as in his whole appearance, in the novelty of this man. His chest was broad and powerful, his hands were slender and well formed, and his graceful, muscular legs were much comelier than Savely's stumps. There could be no comparison, in fact.

"Though I am a long-skirted devil," Savely said after a brief interval, "they've no business to sleep here.... It's government work; we shall have to answer for keeping them. If you carry the letters, carry them, you can't go to sleep.... Hey! you!" Savely shouted into the outer room. "You, driver. What's your name? Shall I show you the way? Get up; postmen mustn't sleep!"

And Savely, thoroughly roused, ran up to the postman and tugged him by the sleeve.

"Hey, your honour, if you must go, go; and if you don't, it's not the thing.... Sleeping won't do."

The postman jumped up, sat down, looked with blank eyes round the hut, and lay down again.

"But when are you going?" Savely pattered away. "That's what the post is for—to get there in good time, do you hear? I'll take you."

The postman opened his eyes. Warmed and relaxed by his first sweet sleep, and not yet quite awake, he saw as through a mist the white neck and the immovable, alluring eyes of the sexton's wife. He closed his eyes and smiled as though he had been dreaming it all.

"Come, how can you go in such weather!" he heard a soft feminine voice; "you ought to have a sound sleep and it would do you good!"

"And what about the post?" said Savely anxiously. "Who's going to take the post? Are you going to take it, pray, you?"

The postman opened his eyes again, looked at the play of the dimples on Raissa's face, remembered where he was, and understood Savely. The thought that he had to go out into the cold darkness sent a chill shudder all down him, and he winced.

"I might sleep another five minutes," he said, yawning. "I shall be late, anyway...."

"We might be just in time," came a voice from the outer room. "All days are not alike; the train may be late for a bit of luck."

The postman got up, and stretching lazily began putting on his coat.

Savely positively neighed with delight when he saw his visitors were getting ready to go.

"Give us a hand," the driver shouted to him as he lifted up a mail-bag.

The sexton ran out and helped him drag the post-bags into the yard. The postman began undoing the knot in his hood. The sexton's wife gazed into his eyes, and seemed trying to look right into his soul.

"You ought to have a cup of tea..." she said.

"I wouldn't say no... but, you see, they're getting ready," he assented. "We are late, anyway."

"Do stay," she whispered, dropping her eyes and touching him by the sleeve.

The postman got the knot undone at last and flung the hood over his elbow, hesitating. He felt it comfortable standing by Raissa.

"What a... neck you've got!..." And he touched her neck with two fingers. Seeing that she did not resist, he stroked her neck and shoulders.

"I say, you are..."

"You'd better stay... have some tea."

"Where are you putting it?" The driver's voice could be heard outside. "Lay it crossways."

"You'd better stay.... Hark how the wind howls."

And the postman, not yet quite awake, not yet quite able to shake off the intoxicating sleep of youth and fatigue, was suddenly overwhelmed by a desire for the sake of which mail-bags, postal trains... and all things in the world, are forgotten. He glanced at the door in a frightened way, as though he wanted to escape or hide himself, seized Raissa round the waist, and was just bending over the lamp to put out the light, when he heard the tramp of boots in the outer room, and the driver appeared in the doorway. Savely peeped in over his shoulder. The postman dropped his hands quickly and stood still as though irresolute.

"It's all ready," said the driver. The postman stood still for a moment, resolutely threw up his head as though waking up completely, and followed the driver out. Raissa was left alone.

"Come, get in and show us the way!" she heard.

One bell sounded languidly, then another, and the jingling notes in a long delicate chain floated away from the hut.

When little by little they had died away, Raissa got up and nervously paced to and fro. At first she was pale, then she flushed all over. Her face was contorted with hate, her breathing was tremulous, her eyes gleamed with wild, savage anger, and, pacing up and down as in a cage, she looked like a tigress menaced with red-hot iron. For a moment she stood still and looked at her abode. Almost half of the room was filled up by the bed, which stretched the length of the whole wall and consisted of a dirty feather-bed, coarse grey pillows, a quilt, and nameless rags of various sorts. The bed was a shapeless ugly mass which suggested the shock of hair that always stood up on Savely's head whenever it occurred to him to oil it. From the bed to the door that led into the cold outer room stretched the dark stove surrounded by pots and hanging clouts. Everything, including the absent Savely himself, was dirty, greasy, and smutty to the last degree, so that it was strange to see a woman's white neck and delicate skin in such surroundings.

Raissa ran up to the bed, stretched out her hands as though she wanted to fling it all about, stamp it underfoot, and tear it to shreds. But then, as though frightened by contact with the dirt, she leapt back and began pacing up and down again.

When Savely returned two hours later, worn out and covered with snow, she was undressed and in bed. Her eyes were closed, but from the slight tremor that ran over her face he guessed that she was not asleep. On his way home he had vowed inwardly to wait till next day and not to touch her, but he could not resist a biting taunt at her.

"Your witchery was all in vain: he's gone off," he said, grinning with malignant joy.

His wife remained mute, but her chin quivered. Savely undressed slowly, clambered over his wife, and lay down next to the wall.

"To-morrow I'll let Father Nikodim know what sort of wife you are!" he muttered, curling himself up.

Raissa turned her face to him and her eyes gleamed.

"The job's enough for you, and you can look for a wife in the forest, blast you!" she said. "I am no wife for you, a clumsy lout, a slug-a-bed, God forgive me!"

"Come, come... go to sleep!"

"How miserable I am!" sobbed his wife. "If it weren't for you, I might have married a merchant or some gentleman! If it weren't for you, I should love my husband now! And you haven't been buried in the snow, you haven't been frozen on the highroad, you Herod!"

Raissa cried for a long time. At last she drew a deep sigh and was still. The storm still raged without. Something wailed in the stove, in the chimney, outside the walls, and it seemed to Savely that the wailing was within him, in his ears. This evening had completely confirmed him in his suspicions about his wife. He no longer doubted that his wife, with the aid of the Evil One, controlled the winds and the post sledges. But to add to his grief, this mysteriousness, this supernatural, weird power gave the woman beside him a peculiar, incomprehensible charm of which he had not been conscious before. The fact that in his stupidity he unconsciously threw a poetic glamour over her made her seem, as it were, whiter, sleeker, more unapproachable.

"Witch!" he muttered indignantly. "Tfoo, horrid creature!"

Yet, waiting till she was quiet and began breathing evenly, he touched her head with his finger... held her thick plait in his hand for a minute. She did not feel it. Then he grew bolder and stroked her neck.

"Leave off!" she shouted, and prodded him on the nose with her elbow with such violence that he saw stars before his eyes.

The pain in his nose was soon over, but the torture in his heart remained.

By Anton Chekhov

LOIS THE WITCH

Elizabeth Gaskell

Chapter 1

In the year 1691, Lois Barclay stood on a little wooden pier, steadying herself on the stable land, in much the same manner as, eight or nine weeks ago, she had tried to steady herself on the deck of the rocking ship which had carried her across from Old to New England. It seemed as strange now to be on solid earth as it had been, not long ago, to be rocked by the sea, both by day and by night; and the aspect of the land was equally strange. The forests which showed in the distance all round, and which, in truth, were not very far from the wooden houses forming the town of Boston, were of different shades of green, and different, too, in shape of outline to those which Lois Barclay knew well in her old home in Warwickshire. Her heart sank a little as she stood alone, waiting for the captain of the good ship Redemption, the kind rough old sailor, who was her only known friend in this unknown continent. Captain Holdernesse was busy, however, as she saw, and it would probably be some time before he would be ready to attend, to her; so Lois sat down on one of the casks that lay about, and wrapped her grey duffle cloak tight around her, and sheltered herself under her hood, as well as might be, from the piercing wind, which seemed to follow those whom it had tyrannized over at sea with a dogged wish of still tormenting them on land. Very patiently did Lois sit there, although she was weary, and shivering with cold; for the day was severe for May, and the Redemption, with store of necessaries and comforts for the Puritan colonists of New England, was the earliest ship that had ventured across the seas.

How could Lois help thinking of the past, and speculating on the future, as she sat on Boston pier, at this breathing-time of her life? In the dim sea-mist which she gazed upon with aching eyes (filled, against her will, with tears, from time to time), there rose the little village church of Barford (not three miles from Warwick—you may see it yet), where her father had preached ever since 1661, long before she was born. He and her mother both lay dead in Barford churchyard; and the old low grey church could hardly come before her vision without her seeing the old parsonage too, the cottage covered with Austrian roses, and yellow jessamine, where she had been born, sole child of parents already long past the prime of youth. She saw the path, not a hundred yards long, from the parsonage to the vestry door: that path which her father trod daily; for the vestry was his study, and the sanctum, where he pored over the ponderous tomes of the Father, and compared their precepts with those of the authorities of the Anglican Church of that day—the day of the later Stuarts; for Barford Parsonage at that time scarcely exceeded in size and dignity the cottages by which it was surrounded: it only contained three rooms on a floor, and was but two stories high. On the first, or ground floor, were the parlour, kitchen, and back or working kitchen; up-stairs, Mr. and Mrs. Barclay's room, that belonging to Lois, and the maid-servant's room. If a guest came, Lois left her own chamber, and shared old Clemence's bed. But those days were over. Never more should Lois see father or mother on earth; they slept, calm and still, in Barford churchyard, careless of what became of their orphan child, as far as earthly manifestations of care or love went. And Clemence lay there too, bound down in her grassy bed by withes of the briar-rose, which Lois had trained over those three precious graves before leaving England for ever.

There were some who would fain have kept her there; one who swore in his heart a great oath unto the Lord that he would seek her sooner or later, if she was still upon the earth. But he was the rich heir and only son of the Miller Lucy, whose mill stood by the Avon-side in the grassy Barford meadows, and his father looked higher for him than the penniless daughter of Parson Barclay (so low were clergymen esteemed in those days!); and the very suspicion of Hugh Lucy's attachment to Lois Barclay made his parents think it more prudent not to offer the orphan a home, although none other of the parishioners had the means, even if they had the will, to do so.

So Lois swallowed her tears down till the time came for crying, and acted upon her mother's words:

'Lois, thy father is dead of this terrible fever, and I am dying. Nay, it is so, though I am easier from pain for these few hours, the Lord be praised! The cruel men of the Commonwealth have left thee very friendless. Thy father's only brother was shot down at Edgehill. I, too, have a brother, though thou hast never heard me speak of him, for he was a schismatic; and thy father and he had words, and he left for that new country beyond the seas, without ever saying farewell to us. But Ralph was a kind lad until he took up these new-fangled notions, and for the old days' sake he will take thee in, and love thee as a child, and place thee among his children. Blood is thicker than water. Write to him as soon as I am gone—for Lois, I am going—and I bless the Lord that has letten me join my husband again so soon.' Such was the selfishness of conjugal love; she thought little of Lois's desolation in comparison with her rejoicing over her speedy reunion with her dead husband! 'Write to thine uncle, Ralph Hickson, Salem, New England (put it down, child, on thy tablets), and say that I, Henrietta Barclay, charge him, for the sake of all he holds dear in heaven or on earth,—for his salvation's sake, as well as for the sake of the old home at Lester-bridge,—for the sake of the father and mother that gave us birth, as well as for the sake of the six little children who lie dead between him and me,—that he take thee into his home as if thou wert his own flesh and blood, as indeed thou art. He has a wife and children of his own, and no one need fear having thee, my Lois, my darling, my baby, among his household. Oh, Lois, would that thou wert dying with me! The thought of thee makes death sore!' Lois comforted her mother more than herself, poor child, by promises to obey her dying wishes to the letter, and by expressing hopes she dared not feel of her uncle's kindness.

'Promise me'—the dying woman's breath came harder and harder—'that thou wilt go at once. The money our goods will bring—the letter thy father wrote to Captain Holdernesse, his old schoolfellow—thou knowest all I would say—my Lois, God bless thee!'

Solemnly did Lois promise; strictly she kept her word. It was all the more easy, for Hugh Lucy met her, and told her, in one great burst of love, of his passionate attachment, his vehement struggles with his father, his impotence at present, his hope and resolves for the future. And, intermingled with all this, came such outrageous threats and expressions of uncontrolled vehemence, that Lois felt that in Barford she must not linger to be a cause of desperate quarrel between father and son, while her absence might soften down matters, so that either the rich old miller might relent, or—and her heart ached to think of the other possibility—Hugh's love might cool, and the dear play-fellow of her childhood learn to forget. If not—if Hugh were to be trusted in one tithe of what he said—God might permit him to fulfil his resolve of coming to seek her out before many years were over. It was all in God's hands, and that was best, thought Lois Barclay.

She was roused out of her trance of recollections by Captain Holdernesse, who, having done all that was necessary in the way of orders and directions to his mate, now came up to her, and, praising her for her quiet patience, told her that he would now take her to the Widow Smith's, a decent kind of house, where he and many other sailors of the better order were in the habit of lodging, during their stay on the New England shores. Widow Smith, he said, had a parlour for herself and her daughters, in which Lois might sit, while he went about the business that, as he had told her, would detain him in Boston for a day or two, before he could accompany her to her uncle's at Salem. All this had been to a certain degree arranged on ship-board; but Captain Holdernesse, for want of anything else that he could think of to talk about, recapitulated it as he and Lois walked along. It was his way of showing sympathy with the emotion that made her grey eyes full of tears, as she started up from the pier at the sound of his voice. In his heart he said, 'Poor wench! poor wench! it's a strange land to her, and they are all strange folks, and, I reckon, she will be feeling desolate. I'll try and cheer her up.' So he talked on about hard facts, connected with the life that lay before her, until they reached Widow Smith's; and perhaps Lois was more brightened by this style of conversation, and the new ideas it presented to her, than she would have been by the tenderest woman's sympathy.

'They are a queer set, these New Englanders,' said Captain Holdernesse. 'They are rare chaps for praying; down on their knees at every turn of their life. Folk are none so busy in a new country, else they would have to pray like me, with a "Yo-hoy!" on each side of my prayers, and a rope cutting like fire through my hand. Yon pilot was for calling us all to thanksgiving for a good voyage, and lucky escape from the pirates; but I said I always put up my thanks on dry land, after I had got my ship into harbour. The French colonists, too, are vowing vengeance for the expedition against Canada, and the people here are raging like heathens—at least, as like as godly folk can be—for the loss of their charter. All that is the news the pilot told me; for, for all he wanted us to be thanksgiving instead of casting the lead, he was as down in the mouth as could be about the state of the country. But here we are at Widow Smith's! Now, cheer up, and show the godly a pretty smiling Warwickshire lass!'

Anybody would have smiled at Widow Smith's greeting. She was a comely, motherly woman, dressed in the primmest fashion in vogue twenty years before, in England, among the class to which she belonged. But, somehow, her pleasant face gave the lie to her dress; were it as brown and sober-coloured as could be, folk remembered it bright and cheerful, because it was a part of Widow Smith herself.

She kissed Lois on both cheeks, before she rightly understood who the stranger maiden was, only because she was a stranger, and looked sad and forlorn; and then she kissed her again, because Captain Holdernesse commended her to the widow's good offices. And so she led Lois by the hand into her rough, substantial log-house, over the door of which hung a great bough of a tree, by way of sign of entertainment for man and horse. Yet not all men were received by Widow Smith. To some she could be as cold and reserved as need be, deaf to all inquiries save one—where else they could find accommodation? To this question she would give a ready answer, and speed the unwelcome guest on his way. Widow Smith was guided in these matters by instinct: one glance at a man's face told her whether or not she chose to have him as an inmate of the same house as her daughters; and her promptness of decision in these matters gave her manner a kind of authority which no one liked to disobey, especially as she had stalwart neighbours within call to back her, if her assumed deafness in the first instance, and her voice and gesture in the second, were not enough to give the would-be guest his dismissal. Widow Smith chose her customers merely by their physical aspect; not one whit with regard to their apparent worldly circumstances. Those who had been staying at her house once, always came again, for she had the knack of making every one beneath her roof comfortable and at his ease. Her daughters, Prudence and Hester, had somewhat of their mother's gifts, but not in such perfection. They reasoned a little upon a stranger's appearance, instead of knowing at the first moment whether they liked him or no; they noticed the indications of his clothes, the quality and cut thereof, as telling somewhat of his station in society; they were more reserved, they hesitated more than their mother; they had not her prompt authority, her happy power. Their bread was not so light, their cream went sometimes to sleep when it should have been turning into butter, their hams were not always 'just like the hams of the old country,' as their mother's were invariably pronounced to be; yet they were good, orderly, kindly girls, and rose and greeted Lois with a friendly shake of the hand, as their mother, with her arm round the stranger's waist, led her into the private room which she called her parlour. The aspect of this room was strange in the English girl's eyes. The logs of which the house was built, showed here and there through the mud plaster, although before both plaster and logs were hung the skins of many curious animals,—skins presented to the widow by many a trader of her acquaintance, just as her sailor guests brought her another description of gift— shells, strings of wampum-beads, sea-birds' eggs, and presents from the old country. The room was more like a small museum of natural history of these days than a parlour; and it had a strange, peculiar, but not unpleasant smell about it, neutralized in some degree by the smoke from the enormous trunk of pinewood which smouldered on the hearth.

The instant their mother told them that Captain Holdernesse was in the outer room, the girls began putting away their spinning-wheel and knitting-needles, and preparing for a meal of some kind; what meal, Lois, sitting there and unconsciously watching, could hardly tell. First, dough was set to rise for cakes; then came out of a corner cupboard—a present from England—an enormous square bottle of a cordial called Golden Wasser; next, a mill for grinding chocolate—a rare unusual treat anywhere at that time; then a great Cheshire cheese. Three venison steaks were cut ready for broiling, fat cold pork sliced up and treacle poured over it, a great pie something like a mince-pie, but which the daughters spoke of with honour as the 'punken-pie,' fresh and salt fish brandered, oysters cooked in various ways. Lois wondered where would be the end of the provisions for hospitably receiving the strangers from the old country. At length everything was placed on the table, the hot food smoking; but all was cool, not to say cold, before Elder Hawkins (an old neighbour of much repute and standing, who had been invited in by Widow Smith to hear the news) had finished his grace, into which was embodied thanksgivings for the past and prayers for the future lives of every individual present, adapted to their several cases, as far as the elder could guess at them from appearances. This grace might not have ended so soon as it did, had it not been for the somewhat impatient drumming of his knife-handle on the table with which Captain Holdernesse accompanied the latter half of the elder's words.

When they first sat down to their meal, all were too hungry for much talking; but as their appetites diminished their curiosity increased, and there was much to be told and heard on both sides. With all the English intelligence Lois was, of course, well acquainted; but she listened with natural attention to all that was said about the new country, and the new people among whom she had come to live. Her father had been a Jacobite, as the adherents of the Stuarts were beginning at this time to be called. His father, again, had been a follower of Archbishop Laud; so Lois had hitherto heard little of the conversation, and seen little of the ways of the Puritans. Elder Hawkins was one of the strictest of the strict, and evidently his presence kept the two daughters of the house considerably in awe. But the widow herself was a privileged person; her known goodness of heart (the effects of which had been experienced by many) gave her the liberty of speech which was tacitly denied to many, under penalty of being esteemed ungodly if they infringed certain conventional limits. And Captain Holdernesse and his mate spoke out their minds, let who would be present. So that on this first landing in New England, Lois was, as it were, gently let down into the midst of the Puritan peculiarities, and yet they were sufficient to make her feel very lonely and strange.

The first subject of conversation was the present state of the colony—Lois soon found out that, although at the beginning she was not a little perplexed by the frequent reference to names of places which she naturally associated with the old country. Widow Smith was speaking: 'In the county of Essex the folk are ordered to keep four scouts, or companies of minute-men; six persons in each company; to be on the look-out for the wild Indians, who are for ever stirring about in the woods, stealthy brutes as they are! I am sure, I got such a fright the first harvest-time after I came over to New England, I go on dreaming, now near twenty years after Lothrop's business, of painted Indians, with their shaven scalps and their war-streaks, lurking behind the trees, and coming nearer and nearer with their noiseless steps.'

'Yes,' broke in one of her daughters; 'and, mother, don't you remember how Hannah Benson told us how her husband had cut down every tree near his house at

Deerbrook, in order that no one might come near him, under cover; and how one evening she was a-sitting in the twilight, when all her family were gone to bed, and her husband gone off to Plymouth on business, and she saw a log of wood, just like a trunk of a felled tree, lying in the shadow, and thought nothing of it, till, on looking again a while after, she fancied it was come a bit nearer to the house, and how her heart turned sick with fright, and how she dared not stir at first, but shut her eyes while she counted a hundred, and looked again, and the shadow was deeper, but she could see that the log was nearer; so she ran in and bolted the door, and went up to where her eldest lad lay. It was Elijah, and he was but sixteen then; but he rose up at his mother's words, and took his father's long duck-gun down, and he tried the loading, and spoke for the first time to put up a prayer that God would give his aim good guidance, and went to a window that gave a view upon the side where the log lay, and fired, and no one dared to look what came of it, but all the household read the Scriptures, and prayed the whole night long, till morning came and showed a long stream of blood lying on the grass close by the log, which the full sunlight showed to be no log at all, but just a Red Indian covered with bark, and painted most skilfully, with his war-knife by his side.'

All were breathless with listening, though to most the story, or such like it, were familiar. Then another took up the tale of horror:

'And the pirates have been down at Marblehead since you were here, Captain Holdernesse. 'Twas only the last winter they landed,—French Papist pirates; and the people kept close within their houses, for they knew not what would come of it; and they dragged folk ashore. There was one woman among those folk—prisoners from some vessel, doubtless—and the pirates took them by force to the inland marsh; and the Marblehead folk kept still and quiet, every gun loaded, and every ear on the watch, for who knew but what the wild sea-robbers might take a turn on land next; and, in the dead of the night, they heard a woman's loud and pitiful outcry from the marsh, 'Lord Jesu! have mercy on me! Save me from the power of man, O Lord Jesu!' And the blood of all who heard the cry ran cold with terror, till old Nance Hickson, who had been stone-deaf and bedridden for years, stood up in the midst of the folk all gathered together in her grandson's house, and said, that as they, the dwellers in Marblehead, had not had brave hearts or faith enough to go and succour the helpless, that cry of a dying woman should be in their ears, and in their children's ears, till the end of the world. And Nance dropped down dead as soon as she had made an end of speaking, and the pirates set sail from Marblehead at morning dawn; but the folk there hear the cry still, shrill and pitiful, from the waste marshes, "Lord Jesu! have mercy on me! Save me from the power of man, O Lord Jesu!"'

'And by token,' said Elder Hawkins's deep bass voice, speaking with the strong nasal twang of the Puritans (who, says Butler,

"Blasphemed custard through the nose"),

'godly Mr. Noyes ordained a fast at Marblehead, and preached a soul-stirring discourse on the words; "Inasmuch as ye did it not unto one of the least of these, my brethren, ye did it not unto me." But it has been borne in upon me at times, whether the whole vision of the pirates and the cry of the woman was not a device of Satan's to sift the Marblehead folk, and see what fruit their doctrine bore, and so to condemn them in the sight of the Lord. If it were so, the enemy had a great triumph, for assuredly it was no part of Christian men to leave a helpless woman unaided in her sore distress.'

'But, Elder,' said Widow Smith, 'it was no vision; they were real living men who went ashore, men who broke down branches and left their footmarks on the ground.'

'As for that matter, Satan hath many powers, and if it be the day when he is permitted to go about like a roaring lion, he will not stick at trifles, but make his work complete. I tell you, many men are spiritual enemies in visible forms, permitted to roam about the waste places of the earth. I myself believe that these Red Indians are indeed the evil creatures of whom we read in Holy Scripture; and there is no doubt that they are in league with those abominable Papists, the French people in Canada. I have heard tell, that the French pay the Indians so much gold for every dozen scalps off Englishmen's heads.'

'Pretty cheerful talk this,' said Captain Holdernesse to Lois, perceiving her blanched cheek and terror-stricken mien. 'Thou art thinking that thou hadst better have stayed at Barford, I'll answer for it, wench. But the devil is not so black as he is painted.'

'Ho! there again!' said Elder Hawkins. 'The devil is painted, it hath been said so from old times; and are not these Indians painted, even like unto their father?'

'But is it all true?' asked Lois, aside, of Captain Holdernesse, letting the elder hold forth unheeded by her, though listened to, however, with the utmost reverence by the two daughters of the house.

'My wench,' said the old sailor, 'thou hast come to a country where there are many perils, both from land and from sea. The Indians hate the white men. Whether other white men' (meaning the French away to the north) 'have hounded on the savages, or whether the English have taken their lands and hunting-grounds without due recompense, and so raised the cruel vengeance of the wild creatures—who knows? But it is true that it is not safe to go far into the woods, for fear of the lurking painted savages; nor has it been safe to build a dwelling far from a settlement; and it takes a brave heart to make a journey from one town to another, and folk do say the Indian creatures rise up out of the very ground to waylay the English; and then offers affirm they are all in league with Satan to affright the Christians out of the heathen country over which he has reigned so long. Then, again, the seashore is infested by pirates, the scum of all nations: they land, and plunder, and ravage, and burn, and destroy. Folk get affrighted of the real dangers, and in their fright imagine, perchance, dangers that are not. But who knows? Holy Scripture speaks of witches and wizards, and of the power of the Evil One in desert places; and even in the old country we have heard tell of those who have sold their souls for ever for the little power they get for a few years on earth.'

By this time the whole table was silent, listening to the captain; it was just one of those chance silences that sometimes occur, without any apparent reason, and often without any apparent consequence. But all present had reason, before many months had-passed over, to remember the words which Lois spoke in answer, although her voice was low, and she only thought, in the interest of the moment, of being heard by her old friend the captain.

'They are fearful creatures, the witches! and yet I am sorry for the poor old women, whilst I dread them. We had one in Barford, when I was a little child. No one knew whence she came, but she settled herself down in a mud hut by the common side; and there she lived, she and her cat.' (At the mention of the cat, Elder Hawkins shook his head long and gloomily.) 'No one knew how she lived, if it were not on nettles and scraps of oatmeal and such-like food given her more for fear than for pity. She went double, always talking and muttering to herself. Folk said she snared birds and rabbits, in the thicket that came down to her hovel. How it came to pass I cannot say, but many a one fell sick in the village, and much cattle died one spring, when I was near four years old. I never heard much about it, for my father said it was ill talking about such things; I only know I got a sick fright one afternoon, when the maid had gone out for milk and had taken me with her, and we were passing a meadow where the Avon, circling, makes a deep round pool, and there was a crowd of folk, all still—and a still, breathless crowd makes the heart beat worse than a shouting, noisy one. They were all gazing towards the water, and the maid held me up in her arms to see the sight above the shoulders of the people; and I saw old Hannah in the water, her grey hair all streaming down her shoulders, and her face bloody and black with the stones and the mud they had been throwing at her, and her cat tied round her neck. I hid my face, I know, as soon as I saw the fearsome sight, for her eyes met mine as they were glaring with fury—poor, helpless, baited creature!—and she caught the sight of me, and cried out, "Parson's wench, parson's wench, yonder, in thy nurse's arms, thy dad hath never tried for to save me, and none shall save thee when thou art brought up for a witch." Oh! the words rang in my ears, when I was dropping asleep, for years after. I used to dream that I was in that pond, all men hating me with their eyes because I was a witch; and, at times, her black cat used to seem living again, and say over those dreadful words.'

Lois stopped: the two daughters looked at her excitement with a kind of shrinking surprise, for the tears were in her eyes. Elder Hawkins shook his head, and muttered texts from Scripture; but cheerful Widow Smith, not liking the gloomy turn of the conversation, tried to give it a lighter cast by saying, 'And I don't doubt but what the parson's bonny lass has bewitched many a one since, with her dimples and her pleasant ways—eh, Captain Holdernesse? It's you must tell us tales of this young lass' doings in England.'

'Ay, ay,' said the captain, 'there's one under her charms in Warwickshire who will never get the better of it, I'm thinking.'

Elder Hawkins rose to speak; he stood leaning on his hands, which were placed on the table: 'Brethren,' said he, 'I must upbraid you if ye speak lightly; charms and witchcraft are evil things. I trust this maiden hath had nothing to do with them, even in thought. But my mind misgives me at her story. The hellish witch might have power from Satan to infect her mind, she being yet a child, with the deadly sin. Instead of vain talking, I call upon you all to join with me in prayer for this stranger in our land, that her heart may be purged from all iniquity. Let us pray.'

'Come, there's no harm in that,' said the captain; 'but, Elder Hawkins, when you are at work, just pray for us all, for I am afeard there be some of us need purging from iniquity a good deal more than Lois Barclay, and a prayer for a man never does mischief.'

Captain Holdernesse had business in Boston which detained him there for a couple of days, and during that time Lois remained with the Widow Smith, seeing what was to be seen of the new land that contained her future home. The letter of her dying mother was sent off to Salem, meanwhile, by a lad going thither, in order to prepare her Uncle Ralph Hickson for his niece's coming, as soon as Captain Holdernesse could find leisure to take her; for he considered her given into his own personal charge, until he could consign her to her uncle's care. When the time came for going to Salem, Lois felt very sad at leaving the kindly woman under whose roof she had been staying, and looked back as long as she could see anything of

Widow Smith's dwelling. She was packed into a rough kind of country cart, which just held her and Captain Holdernesse, beside the driver. There was a basket of provisions under their feet, and behind them hung a bag of provender for the horse; for it was a good day's journey to Salem, and the road was reputed so dangerous that it was ill tarrying a minute longer than necessary for refreshment. English roads were bad enough at that period and for long after, but in America the way was simply the cleared ground of the forest; the stumps of the felled trees still remaining in the direct line, forming obstacles, which it required the most careful driving to avoid; and in the hollows, where the ground was swampy, the pulpy nature of it was obviated by logs of wood laid across the boggy part. The deep green forest, tangled into heavy darkness even thus early in the year, came within a few yards of the road all the way, though efforts were regularly made by the inhabitants of the neighbouring settlements to keep a certain space clear on each side, for fear of the lurking Indians, who might otherwise come upon them unawares. The cries of strange birds, the unwonted colour of some of them, all suggested to the imaginative or unaccustomed traveller the idea of war-whoops and painted deadly enemies. But at last they drew near to Salem, which rivalled Boston in size in those days, and boasted the name of one or two streets, although to an English eye they looked rather more like irregularly built houses, clustered round the meeting-house, or rather one of the meeting-houses, for a second was in process of building. The whole place was surrounded with two circles of stockades; between the two were the gardens and grazing ground for those who dreaded their cattle straying into the woods, and the consequent danger of reclaiming them.

The lad who drove them flogged his spent horse into a trot, as they went through Salem to Ralph Hickson's house. It was evening, the leisure time for the inhabitants, and their children were at play before the houses. Lois was struck by the beauty of one wee toddling child, and turned to look after it; it caught its little foot in a stump of wood, and fell with a cry that brought the mother out in affright. As she ran out, her eye caught Lois's anxious gaze, although the noise of the heavy wheels drowned the sound of her words of inquiry as to the nature of the hurt the child had received. Nor had Lois time to think long upon the matter, for the instant after, the horse was pulled up at the door of a good, square, substantial wooden house, plastered over into a creamy white, perhaps as handsome a house as any in Salem; and there she was told by the driver that her uncle, Ralph Hickson, lived. In the flurry of the moment she did not notice, but Captain Holdernesse did, that no one came out at the unwonted sound of wheels, to receive and welcome her. She was lifted down by the old sailor, and led into a large room, almost like the hall of some English manor-house as to size. A tall, gaunt young man of three or four and twenty, sat on a bench by one of the windows, reading a great folio by the fading light of day. He did not rise when they came in, but looked at them with surprise, no gleam of intelligence coming into his stern, dark face. There was no woman in the house-place. Captain Holdernesse paused a moment, and then said:

'Is this house Ralph Hickson's?'

'It is,' said the young man, in a slow, deep voice. But he added no word further.

'This is his niece, Lois Barclay,' said the captain, taking the girl's arm, and pushing her forwards. The young man looked at her steadily and gravely for a minute; then rose, and carefully marking the page in the folio which hitherto had lain open upon his knee, said, still in the same heavy, indifferent manner, 'I will call my mother, she will know.'

He opened a door which looked into a warm bright kitchen, ruddy with the light of the fire over which three women were apparently engaged in cooking something, while a fourth, an old Indian woman, of a greenish-brown colour, shrivelled up and bent with apparent age, moved backwards and forwards, evidently fetching the others the articles they required.

'Mother,' said the young man; and having arrested her attention, he pointed over his shoulder to the newly-arrived strangers, and returned to the study of his book, from time to time, however, furtively examining Lois from beneath his dark shaggy eyebrows.

A tall, largely made woman, past middle life, came in from the kitchen, and stood reconnoitring the strangers.

Captain Holdernesse spoke.

'This is Lois Barclay, Master Ralph Hickson's niece.'

'I know nothing of her,' said the mistress of the house, in a deep voice, almost as masculine as her son's.

'Master Hickson received his sister's letter, did he not? I sent it off myself by a lad named Elias Wellcome, who left Boston for this place yester morning.'

'Ralph Hickson has received no such letter. He lies bedridden in the chamber beyond. Any letters for him must come through my hands; wherefore I can affirm with certainty that no such letter has been delivered here. His sister Barclay, she that was Henrietta Hickson, and whose husband took the oaths to Charles Stuart, and stuck by his living when all godly men left theirs———'

Lois, who had thought her heart was dead and cold a minute before at the ungracious reception she had met with, felt words come up into her mouth at the implied insult to her father, and spoke out, to her own and the captain's astonishment:

'They might be godly men who left their churches on that day of which you speak, madam; but they alone were not the godly men, and no one has a right to limit true godliness for mere opinion's sake.'

'Well said, lass,' spoke out the captain, looking round upon her with a kind of admiring wonder, and patting her on the back.

Lois and her aunt gazed into each other's eyes unflinchingly, for a minute or two of silence; but the girl felt her colour coming and going, while the elder woman's never varied; and the eyes of the young maiden were filling fast with tears, while those of Grate Hickson kept on their stare, dry and unwavering.

'Mother!' said the young man, rising up with a quicker motion than any one had yet used in this house, 'it is ill speaking of such matters when my cousin comes first among us. The Lord may give her grace hereafter, but she has travelled from Boston city to-day, and she and this seafaring man must need rest and food.'

He did not attend to see the effect of his words, but sat down again, and seemed to be absorbed in his book in an instant. Perhaps he knew that his word was law with his grim mother, for he had hardly ceased speaking before she had pointed to a wooden settle; and smoothing the lines on her countenance, she said, 'What Manasseh says is true. Sit down here, while I bid Faith and Nattee get food ready; and meanwhile I will go tell my husband, that one who calls herself his sister's child is come over to pay him a visit.'

She went to the door leading into the kitchen, and gave some directions to the elder girl, whom Lois now knew to be the daughter of the house. Faith stood impassive, while her mother spoke, scarcely caring to look at the newly-arrived strangers. She was like her brother Manasseh in complexion, but had handsomer features, and large, mysterious-looking eyes, as Lois saw, when once she lifted them up, and took in, as it were, the aspect of the sea-captain and her cousin with one swift searching look. About the stiff, tall, angular mother, and the scarce less pliant figure of the daughter, a girl of twelve years old, or thereabouts, played all manner of impish antics, unheeded by them, as if it were her accustomed habit to peep about, now under their arms, now at this side, now at that, making grimaces all the while at Lois and Captain Holdernesse, who sat facing the door, weary, and somewhat disheartened by their reception. The captain pulled out tobacco, and began to chew it by way of consolation; but in a moment or two, his usual elasticity of spirit came to his rescue, and he said in a low voice to Lois:

'That scoundrel Elias, I will give it him! If the letter had but been delivered, thou wouldst have had a different kind of welcome; but as soon as I have had some victuals, I will go out and find the lad, and bring back the letter, and that will make all right, my wench. Nay, don't be downhearted, for I cannot stand women's tears. Thou'rt just worn out with the shaking and the want of food.'

Lois brushed away her tears, and looking round to try and divert her thoughts by fixing them on present object, she caught her cousin Manasseh's deep-set eyes furtively watching her. It was with no unfriendly gaze, yet it made Lois uncomfortable, particularly as he did not withdraw his looks after he must have seen that she observed him. She was glad when her aunt called her into an inner room to see her uncle, and she escaped from the steady observance of her gloomy, silent cousin.

Ralph Hickson was much older than his wife, and his illness made him look older still. He had never had the force of character that Grace, his spouse, possessed, and age and sickness had now rendered him almost childish at times. But his nature was affectionate, and stretching out his trembling arms from where he lay bedridden, he gave Lois an unhesitating welcome, never waiting for the confirmation of the missing letter before he acknowledged her to be his niece.

'Oh! 'tis kind in thee to come all across the sea to make acquaintance with thine uncle; kind in Sister Barclay to spare thee!'

Lois had to tell him that there was no one living to miss her at home in England; that in fact she had no home in England, no father nor mother left upon earth; and that she had been bidden by her mother's last words to seek him out, and ask him for a home. Her words came up, half choked from a heavy heart, and his dulled wits could not take their meaning in without several repetitions; and then he cried like a child, rather at his own loss of a sister, whom he had not seen for more than twenty years, than at that of the orphan's standing before him, trying hard not to cry, but to start bravely in this new strange home. What most of all helped Lois in her self-restraint was her aunt's unsympathetic look. Born and bred in New England, Grace Hickson had a kind of jealous dislike to her husband's English relations, which had increased since of late years his weakened mind yearned after them, and he forgot the good reason he had had for his self-exile, and moaned over the decision which had led to it as the great mistake of his life. 'Come,' said she, 'it strikes me that, in all this sorrow for the loss of one who died full of years, ye are forgetting in Whose hands life and death are!'

True words, but ill-spoken at that time. Lois looked up at her with a scarcely disguised indignation; which increased as she heard the contemptuous tone in which her aunt went on talking to Ralph Hickson, even while she was arranging his bed with a regard to his greater comfort.

'One would think thou wert a godless man, by the moan thou art always making over spilt milk; and truth is, thou art but childish in thine old age. When we were wed, thou left all things to the Lord; I would never have married thee else. Nay, lass,' said she, catching the expression on Lois's face, 'thou art never going to browbeat me with thine angry looks. I do my duty as I read it, and there is never a man in Salem that dare speak a word to Grace Hickson about either her works or her faith. Godly Mr. Cotton Mather hath said, that even he might learn of me; and I would advise thee rather to humble thyself, and see if the Lord may not convert thee from thy ways, since he has sent thee to dwell, as it were, in Zion, where the precious dew falls daily on Aaron's beard.'

Lois felt ashamed and sorry to find that her aunt had so truly interpreted the momentary expression of her features; she blamed herself a little for the feeling that had caused that expression, trying to think how much her aunt might have been troubled with something before the unexpected irruption of the strangers, and again hoping that the remembrance of this little misunderstanding would soon pass away. So she endeavoured to reassure herself, and not to give way to her uncle's tender trembling pressure of her hand, as, at her aunt's bidding, she wished him good night, and returned into the outer, or 'keeping'-room, where all the family were now assembled, ready for the meal of flour cakes and venison-steaks which Nattee, the Indian servant, was bringing in from the kitchen. No one seemed to have been speaking to Captain Holdernesse while Lois had been away. Manasseh sat quiet and silent where he did, with the book open upon his knee, his eyes thoughtfully fixed on vacancy, as if he saw a vision, or dreamed dreams. Faith stood by the table, lazily directing Nattee in her preparations; and Prudence lolled against the door-frame, between kitchen and keeping-room, playing tricks on the old Indian woman as she passed backwards and forwards, till Nattee appeared to be in a strong state of expressed irritation, which he tried in vain to repress, as whenever she showed any sign of it, Prudence only seemed excited to greater mischief. When all was ready, Manasseh lifted his right hand, and 'asked a blessing,' as it was termed; but the grace became a long prayer for abstract spiritual blessings, for strength to combat Satan, and to quench his fiery darts, and at length assumed, so Lois thought, a purely personal character, as if the young man had forgotten the occasion, and even the people present, but was searching into the nature of the diseases that beset his own sick soul, and spreading them out before the Lord. He was brought back by a pluck at the coat from Prudence; he opened his shut eyes, cast an angry glance at the child, who made a face at him for sole reply, and then he sat down, and they all fell to. Grace Hickson would have thought her hospitality sadly at fault, if she had allowed Captain Holdernesse to go out in search of a bed. Skins were spread for him on the floor of the keeping-room; a Bible, and a square bottle of spirits were placed on the table, to supply his wants during the night; and in spite of all the cares and troubles, temptations, or sins of the members of that household, they were all asleep before the town clock struck ten.

In the morning, the captain's first care was to go out in search of the boy Elias, and the missing letter. He met him bringing it with an easy conscience, for, thought Elias, a few hours sooner or later will make no difference; to-night or the morrow morning will be all the same. But he was startled into a sense of wrong-doing by a sound box on the ear, from the very man who had charged him to deliver it speedily, and whom he believed to be at that very moment in Boston city.

The letter delivered, all possible proof being given that Lois had a right to claim a home from her nearest relations, Captain Holdernesse thought it best to take leave.

'Thou'lt take to them, lass, maybe, when there is no one here to make thee think on the old country. Nay, nay! parting is hard work at all times, and best get hard work done out of hand. Keep up thine heart, my wench, and I'll come back and see thee next spring, if we are all spared till then; and who knows what fine young miller mayn't come with me? Don't go and get wed to a praying Puritan, meanwhile. There, there—I'm off! God bless thee!'

And Lois was left alone in New England.

Chapter 2

It was hard up-hill work for Lois to win herself a place in this family. Her aunt was a woman of narrow, strong affections. Her love for her husband, if ever she had any, was burnt out and dead long ago. What she did for him she did from duty; but duty was not strong enough to restrain that little member the tongue; and Lois's heart often bled at the continual flow of contemptuous reproof which Grace constantly addressed to her husband, even while she was sparing no pains or trouble to minister to his bodily ease and comfort. It was more as a relief to herself that she spoke in this way, than with any desire that her speeches should affect him; and he was too deadened by illness to feel hurt by them; or, it may be, the constant repetition of her sarcasms had made him indifferent; at any rate, so that he had his food and his state of bodily warmth attended to, he very seldom seemed to care much for anything else. Even his first flow of affection towards Lois was soon exhausted; he cared for her because she arranged his pillows well and skilfully, and because she could prepare new and dainty kinds of food for his sick appetite, but no longer for her as his dead sister's child. Still he did care for her, and Lois was too glad of this little hoard of affection to examine how or why it was given. To him she could give pleasure, but apparently to no one else in that household. Her aunt looked askance at her for many reasons: the first coming of Lois to Salem was inopportune, the expression of disapprobation on her face on that evening still lingered and rankled in Grace's memory, early prejudices, and feelings, and prepossessions of the English girl were all on the side of what would now be called Church and State, what was then esteemed in that country a superstitious observance of the directions of a Popish rubric, and a servile regard for the family of an oppressing and irreligious king. Nor is it to be supposed that Lois did not feel, and feel acutely, the want of sympathy that all those with whom she was now living manifested towards the old hereditary loyalty (religious as well as political loyalty) in which she had been brought up. With her aunt and Manasseh it was more than want of sympathy; it was positive, active antipathy to all the ideas Lois held most dear. The very allusion, however incidentally made, to the little old grey church at Barford, where her father had preached so long,—the occasional reference to the troubles in which her own country had been distracted when she left,—and the adherence, in which she had been brought up, to the notion that the king could do no wrong, seemed to irritate Manasseh past endurance. He would get up from his reading, his constant employment when at home, and walk angrily about the room after Lois had said anything of this kind, muttering to himself; and once he had even stopped before her, and in a passionate tone bade her not talk so like a fool. Now this was very different to his mother's sarcastic, contemptuous way of treating all poor Lois's little loyal speeches. Grace would lead her on—at least she did at first, till experience made Lois wiser—to express her thoughts on such subjects, till, just when the girl's heart was opening, her aunt would turn round upon her with some bitter sneer that roused all the evil feelings in Lois's disposition by its sting. Now Manasseh seemed, through all his anger, to be so really grieved by what he considered her error, that he went much nearer to convincing her that there might be two sides to a question. Only this was a view, that it appeared like treachery to her dead father's memory to entertain.

Somehow, Lois felt instinctively that Manasseh was really friendly towards her. He was little in the house; there was farming, and some kind of mercantile business to be transacted by him, as real head of the house; and as the season drew on, he went shooting and hunting in the surrounding forests, with a daring which caused his mother to warn and reprove him in private, although to the neighbours she boasted largely of her son's courage and disregard of danger. Lois did not often walk out for the mere sake of walking, there was generally some household errand to be transacted when any of the women of the family went abroad; but once or twice she had caught glimpses of the dreary, dark wood, hemming in the cleared land on all sides,—the great wood with its perpetual movement of branch and bough, and its solemn wail, that came into the very streets of Salem when certain winds blew, bearing the sound of the pine-trees clear upon the ears that had leisure to listen. And from all accounts, this old forest, girdling round the settlement, was full of dreaded and mysterious beasts, and still more to be dreaded Indians, stealing in and out among the shadows, intent on bloody schemes against the Christian people; panther-streaked, shaven Indians, in league by their own confession, as well as by the popular belief, with evil powers.

Nattee, the old Indian servant, would occasionally make Lois's blood run cold as she and Faith and Prudence listened to the wild stories she told them of the wizards of her race. It was often in the kitchen, in the darkening evening, while some cooking process was going on, that the old Indian crone, sitting on her haunches by the bright red wood embers which sent up no flame, but a lurid light reversing the shadows of all the faces around, told her weird stories while they were awaiting the rising of the dough, perchance, out of which the household bread had to be made. There ran through these stories always a ghastly, unexpressed suggestion of some human sacrifice being needed to complete the success of any incantation to the Evil One; and the poor old creature, herself believing and shuddering as she narrated her tale in broken English, took a strange, unconscious pleasure in her power over her hearers—young girls of the oppressing race, which had brought her down into a state little differing from slavery, and reduced her people to outcasts on the hunting-grounds which had belonged to her fathers. After such tales, it required no small effort on Lois's part to go out, at her aunt's command, into the common pasture round the town, and bring the cattle home at night. Who knew but what the double-headed snake might start up from each blackberry-bush—that wicked, cunning, accursed creature in the service of the Indian wizards, that had such power over all those white maidens who met the eyes placed at either end of his long, sinuous, creeping body, so that loathe him, loathe the Indian race as they would, off they must go into the forest to seek but some Indian man, and must beg to be taken into his wigwam, abjuring faith and race for ever? Or there were spells—so Nattee said—hidden about the ground by the wizards, which changed that person's nature who found them; so that, gentle and loving as they might have been before, thereafter they took no pleasure but in the cruel torments of others, and had a strange power given to them of causing such torments at their will. Once Nattee, speaking low to Lois, who was alone with her in the kitchen, whispered out her terrified belief that such a spell had Prudence found; and when the Indian showed her arms to Lois, all pinched and black and blue by the impish child, the English girl began to be afraid of her cousin as of one possessed. But it was not Nattee alone, nor young imaginative girls alone, that believed in these stories. We can afford to smile at them now; but our English ancestors entertained superstitions of much the same character at the same period, and with less excuse, as the circumstances surrounding them were better known, and consequently more explicable by common sense than the real mysteries of the deep, untrodden forests of New England. The gravest divines not only believed stories similar to that of the double-headed serpent, and other tales of witchcraft, but they made such narrations the subjects of preaching and prayer; and as cowardice makes us all cruel, men who were blameless in many of the relations of life, and even praiseworthy in some, became, from superstition, cruel persecutors about this time, showing no mercy towards any one whom they believed to be in league with the Evil One.

Faith was the person with whom the English girl was the most intimately associated in her uncle's house. The two were about the same age, and certain household employments were shared between them. They took it in turns to call in the cows, to make up the butter which had been churned by Hosea, a stiff old out-door servant, in whom Grace Hickson placed great confidence; and each lassie had her great spinning-wheel for wool, and her lesser for flax, before a month had elapsed after Lois's coming. Faith was a grave, silent person, never merry, sometimes very sad, though Lois was a long time in even guessing why. She would try in her sweet, simple fashion to cheer her cousin up, when the latter was depressed, by telling her old stories of English ways and life. Occasionally, Faith seemed to care to listen, occasionally she did not heed one word, but dreamed on. Whether of the past or of the future, who could tell?

Stern old ministers came in to pay their pastoral visits. On such occasions, Grace Hickson would put on clean apron and clean cap, and make them more welcome than she was ever seen to do no one else, bringing out the best provisions of her store, and setting of all before them. Also, the great Bible was brought forth, and Hosea and Nattee summoned from their work to listen while the minister read a chapter, and, as he read, expounded it at considerable length. After this all knelt, while he, standing, lifted up his right hand, and prayed for all possible combinations of Christian men, for all possible cases of spiritual need; and lastly, taking the individuals before him, he would put up a very personal supplication for each, according to his notion of their wants. At first Lois wondered at the aptitude of one or two prayers of this description to the outward circumstances of each case; but when she perceived that her aunt had usually a pretty long confidential conversation with the minister in the early part of his visit, she became aware that he received both his impressions and his knowledge through the medium of 'that godly woman, Grace Hickson;' and I am afraid she paid less regard to the prayer 'for the maiden from another land, who hath brought the errors of that land as a seed with her, even across the great ocean, and who is letting even now the little seeds shoot up into an evil tree, in which all unclean creatures may find shelter.'

'I like the prayers of our Church better,' said Lois, one day to Faith. 'No clergyman in England can pray his own words, and therefore it is that he cannot judge of others so as to fit his prayers to what he esteems to be their case, as Mr. Tappau did this morning.'

'I hate Mr. Tappau!' said Faith, shortly, a passionate flash of light coming out of her dark, heavy eyes.

'Why so cousin? It seems to me as if he were a good man, although I like not his prayers.'

Faith only repeated her words, 'I hate him.'

Lois was sorry for this strong bad feeling; instinctively sorry, for she was loving herself, delighted in being loved, and felt a jar run through her at every sign of want of love in others. But she did not know what to say, and was silent at the time. Faith, too, went on turning her wheel with vehemence, but spoke never a word until her thread snapped, and then she pushed the wheel away hastily and left the room.

Then Prudence crept softly up to Lois's side. This strange child seemed to be tossed about by varying moods: to-day she was caressing and communicative, to-morrow she might be deceitful, mocking, and so indifferent to the pain or sorrows of others that you could call her almost inhuman.

'So thou dost not like Pastor Tappau's prayers?' she whispered.

Lois was sorry to have been overheard, but she neither would nor could take back her words.

'I like them not so well as the prayers I used to hear at home.'

'Mother says thy home was with the ungodly. Nay, don't look at me so—it was not I that said it. I'm none so fond of praying myself, nor of Pastor Tappau for that matter. But Faith cannot abide him, and I know why. Shall I tell thee, cousin Lois?'

'No! Faith did not tell me, and she was the right person to give her own reasons.'

'Ask her where young Mr. Nolan is gone to, and thou wilt hear. I have seen Faith cry by the hour together about Mr. Nolan.'

'Hush, child, hush!' said Lois, for she heard Faith's approaching step, and feared lest she should overhear what they were saying.

The truth was that, a year or two before, there had been a great struggle in Salem village, a great division in the religious body, and Pastor Tappau had been the leader of the more violent, and, ultimately, the successful party. In consequence of this, the less popular minister, Mr. Nolan, had had to leave the place. And him Faith Hickson loved with all the strength of her passionate heart, although he never was aware of the attachment he had excited, and her own family were too regardless of manifestations of mere feeling to ever observe the signs of any emotion on her part. But the old Indian servant Nattee saw and observed them all. She knew, as well as if she had been told the reason, why Faith had lost all care about father or mother, brother and sister, about household work and daily occupation, nay, about the observances of religion as well. Nattee read the meaning of the deep smouldering of Faith's dislike to Pastor Tappau aright; the Indian woman understood why the girl (whom alone of all the white people she loved) avoided the old minister,—would hide in the wood-stack sooner than be called in to listen to his exhortations and prayers. With savage, untutored people, it is not 'Love me, love my dog,' they are often jealous of the creature beloved; but it is, 'Whom thou hatest I will hate;' and Nattee's feeling towards Pastor Tappau was even an exaggeration of the mute unspoken hatred of Faith.

For a long time, the cause of her cousin's dislike and avoidance of the minister was a mystery to Lois; but the name of Nolan remained in her memory whether she would or no, and it was more from girlish interest in a suspected love affair, than from any indifferent and heartless curiosity, that she could not help piecing together little speeches and actions, with Faith's interest in the absent banished minister, for an explanatory clue, till not a doubt remained in her mind. And this without any further communication with Prudence, for Lois declined hearing any more on the subject from her, and so gave deep offence.

Faith grew sadder and duller as the autumn drew on. She lost her appetite, her brown complexion became sallow and colourless, her dark eyes looked hollow and wild. The first of November was near at hand. Lois, in her instinctive, well-intentioned efforts to bring some life and cheerfulness into the monotonous household, had been telling Faith of many English customs, silly enough, no doubt, and which scarcely lighted up a flicker of interest in the American girl's mind. The cousins were lying awake in their bed in the great unplastered room, which was in part store-room, in part bedroom. Lois was full of sympathy for Faith that night. For long she had listened to her cousin's heavy, irrepressible sighs, in silence. Faith sighed because her grief was of too old a date for violent emotion or crying. Lois listened without speaking in the dark, quiet night hours, for a long, long time. She kept quite still, because she thought such vent for sorrow might relieve her cousin's weary heart. But when at length, instead of lying motionless, Faith seemed to be growing restless even to convulsive motions of her limbs, Lois began to speak, to talk about England, and the dear old ways at home, without exciting much attention on Faith's part, until at length she fell upon the subject of Hallow-e'en, and told about customs then and long afterwards practised in England, and that have scarcely yet died out in Scotland. As she told of tricks she had often played, of the apple eaten facing a mirror, of the dripping sheet, of the basins of water, of the nuts burning side by side, and many other such innocent ways of divination, by which laughing, trembling English maidens sought to see the form of their future husbands, if husbands they were to have, then Faith listened breathlessly, asking short, eager questions, as if some ray of hope had entered into her gloomy heart. Lois went on speaking, telling her of all the stories that would confirm the truth of the second sight vouchsafed to all seekers in the accustomed methods, half believing, half incredulous herself, but desiring, above all things, to cheer up poor Faith.

Suddenly, Prudence rose up from her truckle-bed in the dim corner of the room. They had not thought that she was awake, but she had been listening long.

'Cousin Lois may go out and meet Satan by the brook-side if she will, but if thou goest, Faith, I will tell mother—ay, and I will tell Pastor Tappau, too. Hold thy stories, Cousin Lois, I am afeard of my very life. I would rather never be wed at all, than feel the touch of the creature that would take the apple out of my hand, as I held it over my left shoulder.' The excited girl gave a loud scream of terror at the image her fancy had conjured up. Faith and Lois sprang out towards her, flying across the moonlit room in their white nightgowns. At the same instant, summoned by the same cry, Grace Hickson came to her child.

'Hush! hush!' said Faith, authoritatively.

'What is it, my wench?' asked Grace. While Lois, feeling as if she had done all the mischief, kept silence.

'Take her away, take her away!' screamed Prudence. 'Look over her shoulder—her left shoulder—the Evil One is there now, I see him stretching over for the half-bitten apple.'

'What is this she says?' said Grace, austerely.

'She is dreaming,' said Faith; 'Prudence, hold thy tongue.' And she pinched the child severely, while Lois more tenderly tried to soothe the alarms she felt that she had conjured up.

'Be quiet, Prudence,' said she, 'and go to sleep. I will stay by thee till thou hast gone off into slumber.'

'No, go! go away,' sobbed Prudence, who was really terrified at first, but was now assuming more alarm: than she felt, if from the pleasure she received at perceiving herself the centre of attention. 'Faith shall stay by me, not you, wicked English witch!'

So Faith sat by her sister; and Grace, displeased and perplexed, withdrew to her own bed, purposing to inquire more into the matter in the morning. Lois only hoped it might all be forgotten by that time, and resolved never to talk again of such things. But an event happened in the remaining hours of the night to change the current of affairs. While Grace had been absent from her room, her husband had had another paralytic stroke: whether he, too, had been alarmed by that eldritch scream no one could ever know. By the faint light of the rush candle burning at the bedside, his wife perceived that a great change had taken place in his aspect on her return: the irregular breathing came almost like snorts—the end was drawing near. The family were roused, and all help given that either the doctor or experience could suggest. But before the late November morning light, all was ended for Ralph Hickson.

The whole of the ensuing day, they sat or moved in darkened rooms, and spoke few words, and those below their breath. Manasseh kept at home, regretting his father, no doubt, but showing little emotion. Faith was the child that bewailed her loss most grievously; she had a warm heart, hidden away somewhere under her moody exterior, and her father had shown her far more passive kindness than ever her mother had done, for Grace made distinct favourites of Manasseh, her only son, and Prudence, her youngest child. Lois was about as unhappy as any of them, for she had felt strongly drawn towards her uncle as her kindest friend, and the sense of his loss renewed the old sorrow she had experienced at her own parents' death. But she had no time and no place to cry in. On her devolved many of the cares, which it would have seemed indecorous in the nearer relatives to interest themselves in enough to take an active part: the change required in their dress, the household preparations for the sad feast of the funeral—Lois had to arrange all under her aunt's stern direction.

But a day or two afterwards—the last day before the funeral—she went into the yard to fetch in some fagots for the oven; it was a solemn, beautiful, starlit evening, and some sudden sense of desolation in the midst of the vast universe thus revealed touched Lois's heart, and she sat down behind the woodstack, and cried very plentiful tears.

She was startled by Manasseh, who suddenly turned the corner of the stack, and stood before her.

'Lois crying!'

'Only a little,' she said, rising up, and gathering her bundle of fagots, for she dreaded being questioned by her grim, impassive cousin. To her surprise, he laid his hand on her arm, and said:

'Stop one minute. Why art thou crying, cousin?'

'I don't know,' she said, just like a child questioned in like manner; and she was again on the point of weeping.

'My father was very kind to thee, Lois; I do not wonder that thou grievest after him. But the Lord who taketh away can restore tenfold. I will be as kind as my father—yea, kinder. This is not a time to talk of marriage and giving in marriage. But after we have buried our dead, I wish to speak to thee.'

Lois did not cry now, but she shrank with affright. What did her cousin mean? She would far rather that he had been angry with her for unreasonable grieving, for folly.

She avoided him carefully—as carefully as she could, without seeming to dread him—for the next few days. Sometimes she thought it must have been a bad dream; for if there had been no English lover in the case, no other man in the whole world, she could never have thought of Manasseh as her husband; indeed, till now, there had been nothing in his words or actions to suggest such an idea. Now it had been suggested, there was no telling how much she loathed him. He might be good, and pious—he doubtless was—but his dark fixed eyes, moving so slowly and heavily, his lank black hair, his grey coarse skin, all made her dislike him now—all his personal ugliness and ungainliness struck on her senses with a jar, since those few words spoken behind the haystack.

She knew that sooner or later the time must come for further discussion of this subject; but, like a coward, she tried to put it off, by clinging to her aunt's apron-string, for she was sure that Grace Hickson had far different views for her only son. As, indeed, she had, for she was an ambitious, as well as a religious woman; and by an early purchase of land in Salem village, the Hicksons had become wealthy people, without any great exertions of their own; partly, also, by the silent process of accumulation, for they had never cared to change their manner of living from the time when it had been suitable to a far smaller income than that which they at present enjoyed. So much for worldly circumstances. As for their worldly character, it stood as high. No one could say a word against any of their habits or actions. The righteousness and godliness were patent to every one's eyes. So Grace Hickson thought herself entitled to pick and choose among the maidens, before she should meet with one fitted to be Manasseh's wife. None in Salem came up to her imaginary standard. She had it in her mind even at this very time—so soon after her husband's death—to go to Boston, and take counsel with the leading ministers there, with worthy Mr. Cotton Mather at their head, and see if they could tell her of a well-favoured and godly young maiden in their congregations worthy of being the wife of her son. But, besides good looks and godliness, the wench must have good birth, and good wealth, or Grace Hickson would have put her contemptuously on one side. When once this paragon was found, the ministers had approved, Grace anticipated no difficulty on her son's part. So Lois was right in feeling that her aunt would dislike any speech of marriage between Manasseh and herself.

But the girl was brought to bay one day in this wise. Manasseh had ridden forth on some business, which every one said would occupy him the whole day; but, meeting the man with whom he had to transact his affairs, he returned earlier than any one expected. He missed Lois from the keeping-room where his sisters were spinning, almost immediately. His mother sat by at her knitting—he could see Nattee in the kitchen through the open door. He was too reserved to ask where Lois was, but he quietly sought till he found her—in the great loft, already piled with winter stores of fruit and vegetables. Her aunt had sent her there to examine the apples one by one, and pick out such as were unsound, for immediate use. She was stooping down, and intent upon this work, and was hardly aware of his approach, until she lifted up her head and saw him standing close before her. She dropped the apple she was holding, went a little paler than her wont, and faced him in silence.

'Lois,' he said, 'thou rememberest the words that I spoke while we yet mourned over my father. I think that I am called to marriage now, as the head of this household. And I have seen no maiden so pleasant in my sight as thou art, Lois!' He tried to take her hand. But she put it behind her with a childish shake of her head, and, half-crying, said:

'Please, Cousin Manasseh, do not say this to me. I dare say you ought to be married, being the head of the household now; but I don't want to be married. I would rather not.'

'That is well spoken,' replied he, frowning a little, nevertheless. 'I should not like to take to wife an over-forward maiden, ready to jump at wedlock. Besides, the congregation might talk, if we were to be married too soon after my father's death. We have, perchance, said enough, even now. But I wished thee to have thy mind set at ease as to thy future well-doing. Thou wilt have leisure to think of it, and to bring thy mind more fully round to it.' Again he held out his hand. This time she took hold of it with a free, frank gesture.

'I owe you somewhat for your kindness to me ever since I came, Cousin Manasseh; and I have no way of paying you but by telling you truly I can love you as a dear friend, if you will let me, but never as a wife.'

He flung her hand away, but did not take his eyes off her face, though his glance was lowering and gloomy. He muttered something which she did not quite hear, and so she went on bravely although she kept trembling a little, and had much ado to keep from crying.

'Please let me tell you all. There was a young man in Barford—nay, Manasseh, I cannot speak if you are so angry; it is hard work to tell you any how—he said that he wanted to marry me; but I was poor, and his father would have none of it, and I do not want to marry any one; but if I did, it would be—' Her voice dropped, and her blushes told the rest. Manasseh stood looking at her with sullen, hollow eyes, that had a glittering touch of wilderness in them, and then he said:

'It is borne in upon me—verily I see it as in a vision—that thou must be my spouse, and no other man's. Thou canst not escape what is foredoomed. Months ago, when I set myself to read the old godly books in which my soul used to delight until thy coming, I saw no letters of printers' ink marked on the page, but I saw a gold and ruddy type of some unknown language, the meaning whereof was whispered into my soul; it was, "Marry Lois! marry Lois!" And when my father died, I knew it was the beginning of the end. It is the Lord's will, Lois, and thou canst not escape from it.' And again he would have taken her hand and drawn her towards him. But this time she eluded him with ready movement.

'I do not acknowledge it be the Lord's will, Manasseh,' said she. 'It is not "borne in upon me," as you Puritans call it, that I am to be your wife. I am none so set upon wedlock as to take you, even though there be no other chance for me. For I do not care for you as I ought to care for my husband. But I could have cared for you very much as a cousin—as a kind cousin.'

She stopped speaking; she could not choose the right words with which to speak to him of her gratitude and friendliness, which yet could never be any feeling nearer and dearer, no more than two parallel lines can ever meet.

But he was so convinced, by what he considered the spirit of prophecy, that Lois was to be his wife, that he felt rather more indignant at what he considered to be her resistance to the preordained decree, than really anxious as to the result. Again he tried to convince her that neither he nor she had any choice in the matter, by saying:

'The voice said unto me "Marry Lois," and I said, "I will, Lord."'

'But,' Lois replied, 'the voice, as you call it, has never spoken such a word to me.'

'Lois,' he answered, solemnly, 'it will speak. And then wilt thou obey, even as Samuel did?'

'No, indeed I cannot!' she answered, briskly. 'I may take a dream to be truth, and hear my own fancies, if I think about them too long. But I cannot marry any one from obedience.'

'Lois, Lois, thou art as yet unregenerate; but I have seen thee in a vision as one of the elect, robed in white. As yet thy faith is too weak for thee to obey meekly, but it shall not always be so. I will pray that thou mayest see thy preordained course. Meanwhile, I will smooth away all worldly obstacles.'

'Cousin Manasseh! Cousin Manasseh!' cried Lois after him, as he was leaving the room, 'come back. I cannot put it in strong enough words. Manasseh, there is no power in heaven or earth that can make me love thee enough to marry thee, or to wed thee without such love. And this I say solemnly, because it is better that this should end at once.'

For a moment he was staggered; then he lifted up his hands, and said,

'God forgive thee thy blasphemy! Remember Hazael, who said, "Is thy servant a dog, that he should do this great thing?" and went straight and did it, because his evil courses were fixed and appointed for him from before the foundation of the world. And shall not thy paths be laid out among the godly as it hath been foretold to me?'

He went away; and for a minute or two Lois felt as if his words must come true, and that, struggle as she would, hate her doom as she would, she must become his wife; and, under the circumstances, many a girl would have succumbed to her apparent fate. Isolated from all previous connections, hearing no word from England, living in the heavy, monotonous routine of a family with one man for head, and this man esteemed a hero by most of those around him, simply because he was the only man in the family,—these facts alone would have formed strong presumptions that most girls would have yielded to the offers of such a one. But, besides this, there was much to tell upon the imagination in those days, in that place, and time. It was prevalently believed that there were manifestations of spiritual influence—of the direct influence both of good and bad spirits—constantly to be perceived in the course of men's lives. Lots were drawn, as guidance from the Lord; the Bible was opened, and the leaves allowed to fall apart, and the first text the eye fell upon was supposed to be appointed from above a direction. Sounds were heard that could not be accounted for; they were made by the evil spirits not yet banished from the desert places of which they had so long held possession. Sights, inexplicable and mysterious, were dimly seen—Satan, in some shape, seeking whom he might devour. And at the beginning of the long winter season, such whispered tales, such old temptations and hauntings, and devilish terrors, were supposed to be peculiarly rife. Salem was, as it were, snowed up, and left to prey upon itself. The long, dark evenings, the dimly-lighted rooms, the creaking passages, where heterogeneous articles were piled away out of reach of the keen-piercing frost, and where occasionally, in the dead of night, a sound was heard, as of some heavy falling body, when, next morning, everything appeared to be in its right place—so accustomed are we to measure noises by comparison with themselves, and not with the absolute stillness of the night-season—the white mist, coming nearer and nearer to the windows every evening in strange shapes, like phantoms,—all these, and many other circumstances, such as the distant fall of mighty trees in the mysterious forests girdling them round, the faint whoop and cry of some Indian seeking his camp, and unwittingly nearer to the white men's settlement than either he or they would have liked could they have chosen, the hungry yells of the wild beasts approaching the cattle-pens,—these were the things which made that winter life in Salem, in the memorable time of

1691-2, seem strange, and haunted, and terrific to many: peculiarly weird and awful to the English girl in her first year's sojourn in America.

And now imagine Lois worked upon perpetually by Manasseh's conviction that it was decreed that she should be his wife, and you will see that she was not without courage and spirit to resist as she did, steadily, firmly, and yet sweetly. Take one instance out of many, when her nerves were subjected to a shock, slight in relation it is true, but then remember that she had been all day, and for many days, shut up within doors, in a dull light, that at mid-day was almost dark with a long-continued snow-storm. Evening was coming on, and the wood fire was more cheerful than any of the human beings surrounding it; the monotonous whirr of the smaller spinning-wheels had been going on all day, and the store of flax down stairs was nearly exhausted, when Grace Hickson bade Lois fetch down some more from the store-room, before the light so entirely waned away that it could not be found without a candle, and a candle it would be dangerous to carry into that apartment full of combustible materials, especially at this time of hard frost, when every drop of water was locked up and bound in icy hardness. So Lois went, half-shrinking from the long passage that led to the stairs leading up into the storeroom, for it was in this passage that the strange night sounds were heard, which every one had begun to notice, and speak about in lowered tones. She sang, however, as she went, 'to keep her courage up'—sang, however, in a subdued voice, the evening hymn she had so often sung in Barford church:

'Glory to Thee, my God, this night—'

and so it was, I suppose, that she never heard the breathing or motion of any creature near her till, just as she was loading herself with flax to carry down, she heard some one—it was Manasseh—say close to her ear:

'Has the voice spoken yet? Speak, Lois! Has the voice spoken yet to thee—that speaketh to me day and night, "Marry Lois?"'

She started and turned a little sick, but spoke almost directly in a brave, clear manner:

'No! Cousin Manasseh. And it never will.'

'Then I must wait yet longer,' he replied, hoarsely, as if to himself. 'But all submission—all submission.'

At last a break came upon the monotony of the long, dark winter. The parishioners once more raised the discussion whether—the parish extending as it did—it was not absolutely necessary for Pastor Tappau to have help. This question had been mooted once before; and then Pastor Tappau had acquiesced in the necessity, and all had gone on smoothly for some months after the appointment of his assistant, until a feeling had sprung up on the part of the elder minister, which might have been called jealousy of the younger, if so godly a man as Pastor Tappau could have been supposed to entertain so evil a passion. However that might be, two parties were speedily formed, the younger and more ardent being in favour of Mr. Nolan, the elder and more persistent—and, at the time, the more numerous—clinging to the old grey-headed, dogmatic Mr. Tappau, who had married them, baptized their children, and was to them literally as a 'pillar of the church.' So Mr. Nolan left Salem, carrying away with him, possibly, more hearts than that of Faith Hickson's; but certainly she had never been the same creature since.

But now—Christmas, 1691—one or two of the older members of the congregation being dead, and some who were younger men having come to settle in Salem—Mr. Tappau being also older, and, some charitably supposed, wiser—a fresh effort had been made, and Mr. Nolan was returning to labour in ground apparently smoothed over. Lois had taken a keen interest in all the proceedings for Faith's sake,—far more than the latter did for herself, any spectator would have said. Faith's wheel never went faster or slower, her thread never broke, her colour never came, her eyes were never uplifted with sudden interest, all the time these discussions respecting Mr. Nolan's return were going on. But Lois, after the hint given by Prudence, had found a clue to many a sigh and look of despairing sorrow, even without the help of Nattee's improvised songs, in which, under strange allegories, the helpless love of her favourite was told to ears heedless of all meaning, except those of the tender-hearted and sympathetic Lois. Occasionally, she heard a strange chant of the old Indian woman's—half in her own language, half in broken English—droned over some simmering pipkin, from which the smell was, to say the least, unearthly. Once, on perceiving this odour in the keeping-room, Grace Hickson suddenly exclaimed:

'Nattee is at her heathen ways again; we shall have some mischief unless she is stayed.'

But Faith, moving quicker than ordinary, said something about putting a stop to it, and so forestalled her mother's evident intention of going into the kitchen. Faith shut the door between the two rooms, and entered upon some remonstrance with Nattee; but no one could hear the words used. Faith and Nattee seemed more bound together by love and common interest, than any other two among the self-contained individuals comprising this household. Lois sometimes felt as if her presence as a third interrupted some confidential talk between her cousin and the old servant. And yet she was fond of Faith, and could almost think that Faith liked her more than she did either mother, brother, or sister; for the first two were indifferent as to any unspoken feelings, while Prudence delighted in discovering them only to make an amusement to herself out of them.

One day Lois was sitting by herself at her sewing table, while Faith and Nattee were holding one of the secret conclaves from which Lois felt herself to be tacitly excluded, when the outer door opened, and a tall, pale young man, in the strict professional habit of a minister, entered. Lois sprang up with a smile and a look of welcome for Faith's sake, for this must be the Mr. Nolan whose name had been on the tongue of every one for days, and who was, as Lois knew, expected to arrive the day before.

He seemed half surprised at the glad alacrity with which he was received by this stranger: possibly he had not heard of the English girl, who was an inmate in the house where formerly he had seen only grave, solemn, rigid, or heavy faces, and had been received with a stiff form of welcome, very different from the blushing, smiling, dimpled looks that innocently met him with the greeting almost of an old acquaintance. Lois having placed a chair for him, hastened out to call Faith, never doubting but that the feeling which her cousin entertained for the young pastor was mutual, although it might be unrecognised in its full depth by either.

'Faith!' said she, bright and breathless. 'Guess—no,' checking herself to an assumed unconsciousness of any particular importance likely to be affixed to her words, 'Mr. Nolan, the new pastor, is in the keeping-room. He has asked for my aunt and Manasseh. My aunt is gone to the prayer meeting at Pastor Tappau's, and Manasseh is away.' Lois went on speaking to give Faith time, for the girl had become deadly white at the intelligence, while, at the same time, her eyes met the keen, cunning eyes of the old Indian with a peculiar look of half-wondering awe, while Nattee's looks expressed triumphant satisfaction.

'Go,' said Lois, smoothing Faith's hair, and kissing the white, cold cheek, 'or he will wonder why no one comes to see him, and perhaps think he is not welcome.' Faith went without another word into the keeping-room, and shut the door of communication. Nattee and Lois were left together. Lois felt as happy as if some piece of good fortune had befallen herself. For the time, her growing dread of Manasseh's wild, ominous persistence in his suit, her aunt's coldness, her own loneliness, were all forgotten, and she could almost have danced with joy. Nattee laughed aloud, and talked and chuckled to herself: 'Old Indian woman great mystery. Old Indian woman sent hither and thither; go where she is told, where she hears with her ears. But old Indian woman'—and here she drew herself up, and the expression of her face quite changed—'know how to call, and then white man must come; and old Indian have spoken never a word, and white man have hear nothing with his ears.' So, the old crone muttered.

All this time, things were going on very differently in the keeping-room to what Lois imagined. Faith sat stiller even than usual; her eyes downcast, her words few. A quick observer might have noticed a certain tremulousness about her hands, and an occasional twitching throughout all her frame. But Pastor Nolan was not a keen observer upon this occasion; he was absorbed with his own little wonders and perplexities. His wonder was that of a carnal man—who that pretty stranger might be, who had seemed, on his first coming, so glad to see him, but had vanished instantly, apparently not to reappear. And, indeed, I am not sure if his perplexity was not that of a carnal man rather than that of a godly minister, for this was his dilemma. It was the custom of Salem (as we have already seen) for the minister, on entering a household for the visit which, among other people and in other times, would have been termed a 'morning call,' to put up a prayer for the eternal welfare of the family under whose roof-tree he was. Now this prayer was expected to be adapted to the individual character, joys, sorrows, wants, and failings of every member present; and here was he, a young pastor, alone with a young woman, and he thought—vain thoughts, perhaps, but still very natural—that the implied guesses at her character, involved in the minute supplications above described, would be very awkward in a tête-à-tête prayer; so, whether it was his wonder or his perplexity, I do not know, but he did not contribute much to the conversation for some time, and at last, by a sudden burst of courage and impromptu hit, he cut the Gordian knot by making the usual proposal for prayer, and adding to it a request that the household might be summoned. In came Lois, quiet and decorous; in came Nattee, all one impassive, stiff piece of wood,—no look of intelligence or trace of giggling near her countenance. Solemnly recalling each wandering thought, Pastor Nolan knelt in the midst of these three to pray. He was a good and truly religious man, whose name here is the only thing disguised, and played his part bravely in the awful trial to which he was afterwards subjected; and if at the time, before he went through his fiery persecutions, the human fancies which beset all young hearts came across his, we at this day know that these fancies are no sin. But now he prays in earnest, prays so heartily for himself, with such a sense of his own spiritual need and spiritual failings, that each one of his hearers feels as if a prayer and a supplication had gone up for each of them. Even Nattee muttered the few words she knew of the Lord's Prayer; gibberish though the disjointed nouns and verbs might be, the poor creature said them because she was stirred to unwonted reverence. As for Lois, she rose up comforted and strengthened, as no special prayers of Pastor Tappau had ever made her feel. But Faith was sobbing, sobbing aloud, almost hysterically, and made no effort to rise, but lay on her outstretched arms spread out upon the settle. Lois and Pastor Nolan looked at each other for an instant. Then Lois said:

'Sir, you must go. My cousin has not been strong for some time, and doubtless she needs more quiet than she has had to-day.'

Pastor Nolan bowed, and left the house; but in a moment he returned. Half opening the door, but without entering, he said:

'I come back to ask, if perchance I may call this evening to inquire how young Mistress Hickson finds herself?'

But Faith did not hear this; she was sobbing louder than ever.

'Why did you send him away, Lois? I should have been better directly, and it is so long since I have seen him.'

She had her face hidden as she uttered these words, and Lois could not hear them distinctly. She bent her head down by her cousin's on the settle, meaning to ask her to repeat what she had said. But in the irritation of the moment, and prompted possibly by some incipient jealousy, Faith pushed Lois away so violently that the latter was hurt against the hard, sharp corner of the wooden settle. Tears came into her eyes; not so much because her cheek was bruised, as because of the surprised pain she felt at this repulse from the cousin towards whom she was feeling so warmly and kindly. Just for the moment, Lois was as angry as any child could have been; but some of the words of Pastor Nolan's prayer yet rang in her ears, and she thought it would be a shame if she did not let them sink into her heart. She dared not, however, stoop again to caress Faith, but stood quietly by her, sorrowfully waiting, until a step at the outer door caused Faith to rise quickly, and rush into the kitchen, leaving Lois to bear the brunt of the new-comer. It was Manasseh, returned from hunting. He had been two days away, in company with other young men belonging to Salem. It was almost the only occupation which could draw him out of his secluded habits. He stopped suddenly at the door on seeing Lois, and alone, for she had avoided him of late in every possible way.

'Where is my mother?'

'At a prayer meeting at Pastor Tappau's. She has taken Prudence. Faith has left the room this minute. I will call her.' And Lois was going towards the kitchen, when he placed himself between her and the door.

'Lois,' said he, 'the time is going by, and I cannot wait much longer. The visions come thick upon me, and my sight grows clearer and clearer. Only this last night, camping out in the woods, I saw in my soul, between sleeping and waking, the spirit come and offer thee two lots, and the colour of the one was white, like a bride's, and the other was black and red, which is, being interpreted, a violent death. And when thou didst choose the latter the spirit said unto me, 'Come!' and I came, and did as I was bidden. I put it on thee with mine own hands, as it is preordained, if thou wilt not hearken unto the voice and be my wife. And when the black and red dress fell to the ground, thou wert even as a corpse three days old. Now, be advised, Lois, in time. Lois, my cousin, I have seen it in a vision, and my soul cleaveth unto thee—I would fain spare thee.'

He was really in earnest—in passionate earnest; whatever his visions, as he called them, might be, he believed in them, and this belief gave something of unselfishness to his love for Lois. This she felt at this moment, if she had never done so before, and it seemed like a contrast to the repulse she had just met with from his sister. He had drawn near her, and now he took hold of her hand, repeating in his wild, pathetic, dreamy way:

'And the voice said unto me, "Marry Lois!"' And Lois was more inclined to soothe and reason with him than she had ever been before, since the first time of his speaking to her on the subject,—when Grace Hickson—and Prudence entered the room from the passage. They had returned from the prayer meeting by the back way, which had prevented the sound of their approach from being heard.

But Manasseh did not stir or look round; he kept his eyes fixed on Lois, as if to note the effect of his words. Grace came hastily forwards, and lifting up her strong right arm, smote their joined hands in twain, in spite of the fervour of Manasseh's grasp.

'What means this?' said she, addressing herself more to Lois than to her son, anger flashing out of her deep-set eyes.

Lois waited for Manasseh to speak. He seemed, but a few minutes before, to be more gentle and less threatening than he had been of late on this subject, and she did not wish to irritate him. But he did not speak, and her aunt stood angrily waiting for an answer.

'At any rate,' thought Lois, 'it will put an end to the thought in his mind when my aunt speaks out about it.'

'My cousin seeks me in marriage,' said Lois.

'Thee!' and Grace struck out in the direction of her niece with a gesture of supreme contempt. But now Manasseh spoke forth:

'Yea! it is preordained. The voice has said it, and the spirit has brought her to me as my bride.'

'Spirit! an evil spirit then. A good spirit would have chosen out for thee a godly maiden of thine own people, and not a prelatist and a stranger like this girl. A pretty return, Mistress Lois, for all our kindness.'

'Indeed, Aunt Hickson, I have done all I could—Cousin Manasseh knows it—to show him I can be none of his. I have told him,' said she, blushing, but determined to say the whole out at once, 'that I am all but troth-plight to a young man of our own village at home; and, even putting all that on one side, I wish not for marriage at present.'

'Wish rather for conversion and regeneration. Marriage is an unseemly word in the mouth of a maiden. As for Manasseh, I will take reason with him in private; and, meanwhile, if thou hast spoken truly, throw not thyself in his path, as I have noticed thou hast done but too often of late.'

Lois's heart burnt within her at this unjust accusation, for she knew how much she had dreaded and avoided her cousin, and she almost looked to him to give evidence that her aunt's last words were not true. But, instead, he recurred to his one fixed idea, and said:

'Mother, listen! If I wed not Lois, both she and I die within the year. I care not for life; before this, as you know, I have sought for death' (Grace shuddered, and was for a moment subdued by some recollection of past horror); 'but if Lois were my wife I should live, and she would be spared from what is the other lot. That whole vision grows clearer to me day by day. Yet, when I try to know whether I am one of the elect, all is dark. The mystery of Free-Will and Fore-Knowledge is a mystery of Satan's devising, not of God's.'

'Alas, my son! Satan is abroad among the brethren even now; but let the old vexed topics rest. Sooner than fret thyself again, thou shalt have Lois to be thy wife, though my heart was set far differently for thee.'

'No, Manasseh,' said Lois. 'I love you well as a cousin, but wife of yours I can never be. Aunt Hickson, it is not well to delude him so. I say, if ever I marry man, I am troth-plight to one in England.'

'Tush, child! I am your guardian in my dead husband's place. Thou thinkest thyself so great a prize that I would clutch at thee whether or no, I doubt not. I value thee not, save as a medicine for Manasseh, if his mind get disturbed again, as I have noted signs of late.'

This, then, was the secret explanation of much that had alarmed her in her cousin's manner: and if Lois had been a physician of modern times, she might have traced somewhat of the same temperament in his sisters as well—in Prudence's lack of natural feeling and impish delight in mischief, in Faith's vehemence of unrequited love. But as yet Lois did not know, any more than Faith, that the attachment of the latter to Mr. Nolan was not merely unreturned, but even unperceived, by the young minister.

He came, it is true—came often to the house, sat long with the family, and watched them narrowly, but took no especial notice of Faith. Lois perceived this, and grieved over it; Nattee perceived it, and was indignant at it, long before Faith slowly acknowledged it to herself, and went to Nattee the Indian woman, rather than to Lois her cousin, for sympathy and counsel.

'He cares not for me,' said Faith. 'He cares more for Lois's little finger than for my whole body,' the girl moaned out in the bitter pain of jealousy.

'Hush thee, hush thee, prairie bird! How can he build a nest, when the old bird has got all the moss and the feathers? Wait till the Indian has found means to send the old bird flying far away.' This was the mysterious comfort Nattee gave.

Grace Hickson took some kind of charge over Manasseh that relieved Lois of much of her distress at his strange behaviour. Yet at times he escaped from his mother's watchfulness, and in such opportunities he would always seek Lois, entreating her, as of old, to marry him—sometimes pleading his love for her, oftener speaking wildly of his visions and the voices which he heard foretelling a terrible futurity.

We have now to do with events which were taking place in Salem, beyond the narrow circle of the Hickson family; but as they only concern us in as far as they bore down in their consequences on the future of those who formed part of it, I shall go over the narrative very briefly. The town of Salem had lost by death, within a very short time preceding the commencement of my story, nearly all its venerable men and leading citizens—men of ripe wisdom and sound counsel. The people had hardly yet recovered from the shock of their loss, as one by one the patriarchs of the primitive little community had rapidly followed each other to the grave. They had been beloved as fathers, and looked up to as judges in the land. The first bad effect of their loss was seen in the heated dissension which sprang up between Pastor Tappau and the candidate Nolan. It had been apparently healed over; but Mr. Nolan had not been many weeks in Salem, after his second coming, before the strife broke out afresh, and alienated many for life who had till then been bound together by the ties of friendship or relationship. Even in the Hickson family something of this feeling soon sprang up; Grace being a vehement partisan of the elder pastor's more gloomy doctrines, while Faith was a passionate, if a powerless, advocate of Mr. Nolan. Manasseh's growing absorption in his own fancies, and imagined gift of prophecy, making him comparatively indifferent to all outward events, did not tend to either the fulfilment of his visions, or the elucidation of the dark mysterious doctrines over which he had pondered too long for the health either of his mind or body; while Prudence delighted in irritating every one by her advocacy of the views of thinking to which they were most opposed, and retailing every gossiping story to the person most likely to disbelieve, and be indignant at what she told, with an assumed unconsciousness of any such effect to be produced. There was much talk of the congregational difficulties and dissensions being carried up to the general court, and each party naturally hoped that, if such were the course of events, the opposing pastor and that portion of the congregation which adhered to him might be worsted in the struggle.

Such was the state of things in the township when, one day towards the end of the month of February, Grace Hickson returned from the weekly prayer meeting; which it was her custom to attend at Pastor Tappau's house, in a state of extreme excitement. On her entrance into her own house she sat down, rocking her body backwards and forwards, and praying to herself: both Faith and Lois stopped their spinning, in wonder at her agitation, before either of them ventured to address her. At length Faith rose, and spoke:

'Mother, what is it? Hath anything happened of an evil nature?'

The brave, stern, old woman's face was blenched, and her eyes were almost set in horror, as she prayed; the great drops running down her cheeks.

It seemed almost as if she had to make a struggle to recover her sense of the present homely accustomed life, before she could find words to answer:

'Evil nature! Daughters, Satan is abroad,—is close to us. I have this very hour seen him afflict two innocent children, as of old he troubled those who were possessed by him in Judea. Hester and Abigail Tappau have been contorted and convulsed by him and his servants into such shapes as I am afeard to think on; and when their father, godly Mr. Tappau, began to exhort and to pray, their howlings were like the wild beasts of the field. Satan is of a truth let loose amongst us. The girls kept calling upon him as if he were even then present among us. Abigail screeched out that he stood at my very back in the guise of a black man; and truly, as I turned round at her words, I saw a creature like a shadow vanishing, and turned all of a cold sweat. Who knows where he is now? Faith, lay straws across on the door-sill.'

'But if he be already entered in,' asked Prudence, 'may not that make it difficult for him to depart?'

Her mother, taking no notice of her question, went on rocking herself, and praying, till again she broke out into narration:

'Reverend Mr. Tappau says, that only last night he heard a sound as of a heavy body dragged all through the house by some strong power; once it was thrown against his bedroom door, and would, doubtless, have broken it in, if he had not prayed fervently and aloud at that very time; and a shriek went up at his prayer that made his hair stand on end; and this morning all the crockery in the house was found broken and piled up in the middle of the kitchen floor; and Pastor Tappau says, that as soon as he began to ask a blessing on the morning's meal, Abigail and Hester cried out, as if some one was pinching them. Lord, have mercy upon us all! Satan is of a truth let loose.'

'They sound like the old stories I used to hear in Barford,' said Lois, breathless with affright.

Faith seemed less alarmed; but then her dislike to Pastor Tappau was so great, that she could hardly sympathise with any misfortunes that befell him or his family.

Towards evening Mr. Nolan came in. In general, so high did party spirit run, Grace Hickson only tolerated his visits, finding herself often engaged at such hours, and being too much abstracted in thought to show him the ready hospitality which was one of her most prominent virtues. But to-day, both as bringing the latest intelligence of the new horrors sprung up in Salem, and as being one of the Church militant (or what the Puritans considered as equivalent to the Church militant) against Satan, he was welcomed by her in an unusual manner.

He seemed oppressed with the occurrences of the day: at first it appeared to be almost a relief to him to sit still, and cogitate upon them, and his hosts were becoming almost impatient for him to say something more than mere monosyllables, when he began:

'Such a day as this, I pray that I may never see again. It is as if the devils whom our Lord banished into the herd of swine, had been permitted to come again upon the earth. And I would it were only the lost spirits who were tormenting us; but I much fear, that certain of those whom we have esteemed as God's people have sold their souls to Satan, for the sake of a little of his evil power, whereby they may afflict others for a time. Elder Sherringham hath lost this very day a good and valuable horse, wherewith he used to drive his family to meeting, his wife being bedridden.'

'Perchance,' said Lois, 'the horse died of some natural disease.'

'True,' said Pastor Nolan; 'but I was going on to say, that as he entered into his house, full of dolour at the loss of his beast, a mouse ran in before him so sudden that it almost tripped him up, though an instant before there was no such thing to be seen; and he caught at it with his shoe and hit it, and it cried out like a human creature in pain, and straight ran up the chimney, caring nothing for the hot flame and smoke.'

Manasseh listened greedily to all this story, and when it was ended he smote upon his breast, and prayed aloud for deliverance from the power of the Evil One; and he continually went on praying at intervals through the evening, with every mark of abject terror on his face and in his manner—he, the bravest, most daring hunter in all the settlement. Indeed, all the family huddled together in silent fear, scarcely finding any interest in the usual household occupations. Faith and Lois sat with arms entwined, as in days before the former had become jealous of the latter; Prudence asked low, fearful questions of her mother and of the pastor as to the creatures that were abroad, and the ways in which they afflicted others; and when Grace besought the minister to pray for her and her household, he made a long and passionate supplication that none of that little flock might ever so far fall away into hopeless perdition as to be guilty of the sin without forgiveness—the sin of Witchcraft.

Chapter 3

'The sin of witchcraft.' We read about it, we look on it from the outside; but we can hardly realize the terror it induced. Every impulsive or unaccustomed action, every little nervous affection, every ache or pain was noticed, not merely by those around the sufferer, but by the person himself, whoever he might be, that was acting, or being acted upon, in any but the most simple and ordinary manner. He or she (for it was most frequently a woman or girl that was the supposed subject) felt a desire for some unusual kind of food—some unusual motion or rest her hand twitched, her foot was asleep, or her leg had the cramp; and the dreadful question immediately suggested itself, 'Is any one possessing an evil power over me, by the help of Satan?' and perhaps they went on to think, 'It is bad enough to feel that my body can be made to suffer through the power of some unknown evil-wisher to me, but what if Satan gives them still further power, and they can touch my soul, and inspire me with loathful thoughts leading me into crimes which at present I abhor?'

and so on, till the very dread of what might happen, and the constant dwelling of the thoughts, even with horror, upon certain possibilities, or what were esteemed such, really brought about the corruption of imagination at least, which at first they had shuddered at. Moreover, there was a sort of uncertainty as to who might be infected—not unlike the overpowering dread of the plague, which made some shrink from their best-beloved with irrepressible fear. The brother or sister, who was the dearest friend of their childhood and youth, might now be bound in some mysterious deadly pact with evil spirits of the most horrible kind—who could tell? And in such a case it became a duty, a sacred duty, to give up the earthly body which had been once so loved, but which was now the habitation of a soul corrupt and horrible in its evil inclinations. Possibly, terror of death might bring on confession and repentance, and purification. Or if it did not, why away with the evil creature, the witch, out of the world, down to the kingdom of the master, whose bidding was done on earth in all manner of corruption and torture of God's creatures! There were others who, to these more simple, if more ignorant, feelings of horror at witches and witchcraft, added the desire, conscious or unconscious, of revenge on those whose conduct had been in any way displeasing to them. Where evidence takes a supernatural character, there is no disproving it. This argument comes up: 'You have only the natural powers; I have supernatural. You admit the existence of the supernatural by the condemnation of this very crime of witchcraft. You hardly know the limits of the natural powers; how then can you define the supernatural? I say that in the dead of night, when my body seemed to all present to be lying in quiet sleep, I was, in the most complete and wakeful consciousness, present in my body at an assembly of witches and wizards with Satan at their head; that I was by them tortured in my body, because my soul would not acknowledge him as its king; and that I witnessed such and such deeds. What the nature of the appearance was that took the semblance of myself, sleeping quietly in my bed, I know not; but admitting, as you do, the possibility of witchcraft, you cannot disprove my evidence.' This evidence might be given truly or falsely, as the person witnessing believed it or not; but every one must see what immense and terrible power was abroad for revenge. Then, again, the accused themselves ministered to the horrible panic abroad. Some, in dread of death, confessed from cowardice to the imaginary crimes of which they were accused, and of which they were promised a pardon on confession. Some, weak and terrified, came honestly to believe in their own guilt, through the diseases of imagination which were sure to be engendered at such a time as this.

Lois sat spinning with Faith. Both were silent, pondering over the stories that were abroad. Lois spoke first.

'Oh, Faith! this country is worse than ever England was, even in the days of Master Matthew Hopkins, the witch-finder. I grow frightened of every one, I think. I even get afeard sometimes of Nattee!'

Faith coloured a little. Then she asked,

'Why? What should make you distrust the Indian woman?'

'Oh! I am ashamed of my fear as soon as it arises in my mind. But, you know, her look and colour were strange to me when first I came; and she is not a christened woman; and they tell stories of Indian wizards; and I know not what the mixtures are which she is sometimes stirring over the fire, nor the meaning of the strange chants she sings to herself. And once I met her in the dusk, just close by Pastor Tappau's house, in company with Hota, his servant—it was just before we heard of the sore disturbance in his house—and I have wondered if she had aught to do with it.'

Faith sat very still, as if thinking. At last she said:

'If Nattee has powers beyond what you and I have, she will not use them for evil; at least not evil to those whom she loves.'

'That comforts me but little,' said Lois. 'If she has powers beyond what she ought to have, I dread her, though I have done her no evil; nay, though I could almost say she bore me a kindly feeling. But such powers are only given by the Evil One; and the proof thereof is, that, as you imply, Nattee would use them on those who offend her.'

'And why should she not?' asked Faith, lifting her eyes, and flashing heavy fire out of them at the question.

'Because,' said Lois, not seeing Faith's glance, 'we are told to pray for them that despitefully use us, and to do good to them that persecute us. But poor Nattee is not a christened woman. I would that Mr. Nolan would baptize her; it would, maybe, take her out of the power of Satan's temptations.'

'Are you never tempted?' asked Faith, half scornfully; 'and yet I doubt not you were well baptized!'

'True,' said Lois, sadly; 'I often do very wrong, but, perhaps, I might have done worse, if the holy form had not been observed.'

They were again silent for a time.

'Lois,' said Faith, 'I did not mean any offence. But do you never feel as if you would give up all that future life, of which the parsons talk, and which seems so vague and so distant, for a few years of real, vivid blessedness to begin to-morrow—this hour, this minute? Oh! I could think of happiness for which I would willingly give up all those misty chances of heaven——'

'Faith, Faith!' cried Lois, in terror, holding her hand before her cousin's mouth, and looking around in fright. 'Hush! you know not who may be listening; you are putting yourself in his power.'

But Faith pushed her hand away, and said, 'Lois, I believe in him no more than I believe in heaven. Both may exist, but they are so far away that I defy them. Why, all this ado about Mr. Tappau's house—promise me never to tell living creature, and I will tell you a secret.'

'No!' said Lois, terrified. 'I dread all secrets. I will hear none. I will do all that I can for you, cousin Faith, in any way; but just at this time, I strive to keep my life and thoughts within the strictest bounds of godly simplicity, and I dread pledging myself to aught that is hidden and secret.'

'As you will, cowardly girl, full of terrors, which, if you had listened to me, might have been lessened, if not entirely done away with.' And Faith would not utter another word, though Lois tried meekly to entice her into conversation on some other subject.

The rumour of witchcraft was like the echo of thunder among the hills. It had broken out in Mr. Tappau's house, and his two little daughters were the first supposed to be bewitched; but round about, from every quarter of the town, came in accounts of sufferers by witchcraft. There was hardly a family without one of these supposed victims. Then arose a growl and menaces of vengeance from many a household—menaces deepened, not daunted by the terror and mystery of the suffering that gave rise to them.

At length a day was appointed when, after solemn fasting and prayer, Mr. Tappau invited the neighbouring ministers and all godly people to assemble at his house, and unite with him in devoting a day to solemn religious services, and to supplication for the deliverance of his children, and those similarly afflicted, from the power of the Evil One. All Salem poured out towards the house of the minister. There was a look of excitement on all their faces; eagerness and horror were depicted on many, while stern resolution, amounting to determined cruelty, if the occasion arose, was seen on others.

In the midst of the prayer, Hester Tappau, the younger girl, fell into convulsions; fit after fit came on, and her screams mingled with the shrieks and cries of the assembled congregation. In the first pause, when the child was partially recovered, when the people stood around exhausted and breathless, her father, the Pastor Tappau, lifted his right hand, and adjured her, in the name of the Trinity, to say who tormented her. There was a dead silence; not a creature stirred of all those hundreds. Hester turned wearily and uneasily, and moaned out the name of Hota, her father's Indian servant. Hota was present, apparently as much interested as any one; indeed, she had been busying herself much in bringing remedies to the suffering child. But now she stood aghast, transfixed, while her name was caught up and shouted out in tones of reprobation and hatred by all the crowd around her. Another moment and they would have fallen upon the trembling creature and torn her limb from limb—pale, dusky, shivering Hota, half guilty-looking from her very bewilderment. But Pastor Tappau, that gaunt, grey man, lifting himself to his utmost height, signed to them to go back, to keep still while he addressed them; and then he told them, that instant vengeance was not just, deliberate punishment; that there would be need of conviction, perchance of confession—he hoped for some redress for his suffering children from her revelations, if she were brought to confession. They must leave the culprit in his hands, and in those of his brother ministers, that they might wrestle with Satan before delivering her up to the civil power. He spoke well, for he spoke from the heart of a father seeing his children exposed to dreadful and mysterious suffering, and firmly believing that he now held the clue in his hand which should ultimately release them and their fellow-sufferers. And the congregation moaned themselves into unsatisfied submission, and listened to his long, passionate prayer, which he uplifted even while the hapless Hota stood there, guarded and bound by two men, who glared at her like bloodhounds ready to slip, even while the prayer ended in the words of the merciful Saviour.

Lois sickened and shuddered at the whole scene; and this was no intellectual shuddering at the folly and superstition of the people, but tender moral shuddering at the sight of guilt which she believed in, and at the evidence of men's hatred and abhorrence, which, when shown even to the guilty, troubled and distressed her merciful heart. She followed her aunt and cousins out into the open air, with downcast eyes and pale face. Grace Hickson was going home with a feeling of triumphant relief at the detection of the guilty one. Faith alone seemed uneasy and disturbed beyond her wont, for Manasseh received the whole transaction as the fulfilment of a prophecy, and Prudence was excited by the novel scene into a state of discordant high spirits.

'I am quite as old as Hester Tappau,' said she; 'her birthday is in September and mine in October.'

'What has that to do with it?' said Faith, sharply.

'Nothing, only she seemed such a little thing for all those grave ministers to be praying for, and so many folk come from a distance—some from Boston they said—all for her sake, as it were. Why, didst thou see, it was godly Mr. Henwick that held her head when he wriggled so, and old Madam Holbrook had herself helped upon a chair to see the better. I wonder how long I might wriggle, before great and godly folk would take so much notice of me? But, I suppose, that comes of being a pastor's daughter. She'll be so set up there'll be no speaking to her now. Faith! thinkest thou that Hota really had bewitched her? She gave me corn-cakes, the last time I was at Pastor Tappau's, just like any other woman, only, perchance, a trifle more good-natured; and to think of her being a witch after all!'

But Faith seemed in a hurry to reach home, paid no attention to Prudence's talking. Lois hastened on with Faith, for Manasseh was walking alongside of his mother, and she kept steady to her plan of avoiding him, even though she pressed her company upon Faith, who had seemed of late desirous of avoiding her.

That evening the news spread through Salem, that Hota had confessed her sin—had acknowledged that she was a witch. Nattee was the first to hear the intelligence. She broke into the room where the girls were sitting with Grace Hickson, solemnly doing nothing, because of the great prayer-meeting in the morning, and cried out, 'Mercy, mercy, mistress, everybody! take care of poor Indian Nattee, who never do wrong, but for mistress and the family! Hota one bad wicked witch, she say so herself; oh, me! oh me!' and stooping over Faith, she said something in a low, miserable tone of voice, of which Lois only heard the word 'torture.' But Faith heard all, and turning very pale, half accompanied, half led Nattee back to her kitchen.

Presently, Grace Hickson came in. She had been out to see a neighbour; it will not do to say that so godly a woman had been gossiping; and, indeed, the subject of the conversation she had held was of too serious and momentous a nature for me to employ a light word to designate it. There was all the listening to and repeating of small details and rumours, in which the speakers have no concern, that constitutes gossiping; but in this instance, all trivial facts and speeches might be considered to bear such dreadful significance, and might have so ghastly an ending, that such whispers were occasionally raised to a tragic importance. Every fragment of intelligence that related to Mr. Tappau's household was eagerly snatched at; how his dog howled all one long night through, and could not be stilled; how his cow suddenly failed in her milk only two months after she had calved; how his memory had forsaken him one morning, for a minute or two, in repeating the Lord's Prayer, and he had even omitted a clause thereof in his sudden perturbation; and how all these forerunners of his children's strange illness might now be interpreted and understood—this had formed the staple of the conversation between Grace Hickson and her friends. There had arisen a dispute among them at last, as to how far these subjections to the power of the Evil One were to be considered as a judgment upon Pastor Tappau for some sin on his part; and if so, what? It was not an unpleasant discussion, although there was considerable difference of opinion; for as none of the speakers had had their families so troubled, it was rather a proof that they had none of them committed any sin. In the midst of this talk, one, entering in from the street, brought the news that Hota had confessed all—had owned to signing a certain little red book which Satan had presented to her—had been present at impious sacraments—had ridden through the air to Newbury Falls—and, in fact, had assented to all the questions which the elders and magistrates, carefully reading over the confessions of the witches who had formerly been tried in England, in order that they might not omit a single inquiry, had asked of her. More she had owned to, but things of inferior importance, and partaking more of the nature of earthly tricks than of spiritual power. She had spoken of carefully adjusted strings, by which all the crockery in Pastor Tappau's house could be pulled down or disturbed; but of such intelligible malpractices the gossips of Salem took little heed. One of them said that such an action showed Satan's prompting, but they all preferred to listen to the grander guilt of the blasphemous sacraments and supernatural rides. The narrator ended with saying that Hota was to be hung the next morning, in spite of her confession, even although her life had been promised to her if she acknowledged her sin; for it was well to make an example of the first-discovered witch, and it was also well that she was an Indian, a heathen, whose life would be no great loss to the community. Grace Hickson on this spoke out. It was well that witches should perish off the face of the earth, Indian or English, heathen or, worse, a baptized Christian who had betrayed the Lord, even as Judas did, and had gone over to Satan. For her part, she wished that the first-discovered witch had been a member of a godly English household, that it might be seen of all men that religious folk were willing to cut off the right hand, and pluck out the right eye, if tainted with this devilish sin. She spoke sternly and well. The last comer said, that her words might be brought to the proof, for it had been whispered that Hota had named others, and some from the most religious families of Salem, whom she had seen among the unholy communicants at the sacrament of the Evil One. And Grace replied that she would answer for it, all godly folk would stand the proof, and quench all natural affection rather than that such a sin should grow and spread among them. She herself had a weak bodily dread of witnessing the violent death even of an animal; but she would not let that deter her from standing amidst those who cast the accursed creature out from among them on the morrow morning.

Contrary to her wont, Grace Hickson told her family much of this conversation. It was a sign of her excitement on the subject that she thus spoke, and the excitement spread in different forms through her family. Faith was flushed and restless, wandering between the keeping-room and the kitchen, and questioning her mother particularly as to the more extraordinary parts of Hota's confession, as if she wished to satisfy herself that the Indian witch had really done those horrible and mysterious deeds.

Lois shivered and trembled with affright at the narration, and the idea that such things were possible. Occasionally she found herself wandering off into sympathetic thought for the woman who was to die, abhorred of all men, and unpardoned by God, to whom she had been so fearful a traitor, and who was now, at this very time—when Lois sat among her kindred by the warm and cheerful firelight, anticipating many peaceful, perchance happy, morrows—solitary, shivering, panic-stricken, guilty, with none to stand by her and exhort her, shut up in darkness between the cold walls of the town prison. But Lois almost shrank from sympathising with so loathsome an accomplice of Satan, and prayed for forgiveness for her charitable thought; and yet, again, she remembered the tender spirit of the Saviour, and allowed herself to fall into pity, till at last her sense of right and wrong became so bewildered that she could only leave all to God's disposal, and just ask that He would take all creatures and all events into His hands.

Prudence was as bright as if she were listening to some merry story—curious as to more than her mother would tell her—seeming to have no particular terror of witches or witchcraft, and yet to be especially desirous to accompany her mother the next morning to the hanging. Lois shrank from the cruel, eager face of the young girl as she begged her mother to allow her to go. Even Grace was disturbed and perplexed by her daughter's pertinacity.

'No!' said she. 'Ask me no more. Thou shalt not go. Such sights are not for the young. I go, and I sicken at the thoughts of it. But I go to show that I, a Christian woman, take God's part against the devil's. Thou shalt not go, I tell thee. I could whip thee for thinking of it.'

'Manasseh says Hota was well whipped by Pastor Tappau ere she was brought to confession,' said Prudence, as if anxious to change the subject of discussion.

Manasseh lifted up his head from the great folio Bible, brought by his father from England, which he was studying. He had not heard what Prudence said, but he looked up at the sound of his name. All present were startled at his wild eyes, his bloodless face. But he was evidently annoyed at the expression of their countenances.

'Why look ye at me in that manner?' asked he. And his manner was anxious and agitated. His mother made haste to speak:

'It was but that Prudence said something that thou hast told her—that Pastor Tappau defiled his hands by whipping the witch Hota. What evil thought has got hold of thee? Talk to us, and crack not thy skull against the learning of man.'

'It is not the learning of man that I study: it is the word of God. I would fain know more of the nature of this sin of witchcraft, and whether it be, indeed, the unpardonable sin against the Holy Ghost. At times I feel a creeping influence coming over me, prompting all evil thoughts and unheard-of deeds, and I question within myself, "Is not this the power of witchcraft?" and I sicken, and loathe all that I do or say, and yet some evil creature hath the mastery over me, and I must needs do and say what I loathe and dread. Why wonder you, mother, that I, of all men, strive to learn the exact nature of witchcraft, and for that end study the word of God? Have you not seen me when I was, as it were, possessed with a devil?'

He spoke calmly, sadly, but as under deep conviction. His mother rose to comfort him.

'My son,' she said, 'no one ever saw thee do deeds, or heard thee utter words, which any one could say were prompted by devils. We have seen thee, poor lad, with thy wits gone astray for a time, but all thy thoughts sought rather God's will in forbidden places, than lost the clue to them for one moment in hankering after the powers of darkness. Those days are long past; a future lies before thee. Think not of witches or of being subject to the power of witchcraft. I did evil to speak of it before thee. Let Lois come and sit by thee, and talk to thee.'

Lois went to her cousin, grieved at heart for his depressed state of mind, anxious to soothe and comfort him, and yet recoiling more than ever from the idea of ultimately becoming his wife—an idea to which she saw her aunt reconciling herself unconsciously day by day, as she perceived the English girl's power of soothing and comforting her cousin, even by the very tones of her sweet cooing voice.

He took Lois's hand.

'Let me hold it. It does me good,' said he. 'Ah, Lois, when I am by you I forget all my troubles—will the day never come when you will listen to the voice that speaks to me continually?'

'I never hear it, Cousin Manasseh,' she said, softly; 'but do not think of the voices. Tell me of the land you hope to enclose from the forest—what manner of trees grow on it?'

Thus, by simple questions on practical affairs, she led him back, in her unconscious wisdom, to the subjects on which he had always shown strong practical sense. He talked on these with all due discretion till the hour for family prayer came round, which was early in those days. It was Manasseh's place to conduct it, as head of the family; a post which his mother had always been anxious to assign to him since her husband's death. He prayed extempore; and to-night his supplications wandered off into wild, unconnected fragments of prayer, which all those kneeling around began, each according to her anxiety for the speaker, to think would never end. Minutes elapsed, and grew to quarters of an hour, and his words only became more emphatic and wilder, praying for himself alone, and laying bare the recesses of his heart. At length his mother rose, and took Lois by the hand, for she had faith in Lois's power over her son, as being akin to that which the shepherd David, playing on his harp, had over king Saul sitting on his throne. She drew her towards him, where he knelt facing into the circle, with his eyes upturned, and the tranced agony of his face depicting the struggle of the troubled soul within.

'Here is Lois,' said Grace, almost tenderly; 'she would fain go to her chamber.' (Down the girl's face the tears were streaming.) 'Rise, and finish thy prayer in thy closet.'

But at Lois's approach he sprang to his feet,—sprang aside.

'Take her away, mother! Lead me not into temptation. She brings me evil and sinful thoughts. She overshadows me, even in the presence of my God. She is no angel of light, or she would not do this. She troubles me with the sound of a voice bidding me marry her, even when I am at my prayers. Avaunt! Take her away!'

He would have struck at Lois if she had not shrunk back, dismayed and affrighted. His mother, although equally dismayed, was not affrighted. She had seen him thus before; and understood the management of his paroxysm.

'Go, Lois! the sight of thee irritates him, as once that of Faith did. Leave him to me.'

And Lois rushed away to her room, and threw herself on her bed, like a panting, hunted creature. Faith came after her slowly and heavily.

'Lois,' said she, 'wilt thou do me a favour? It is not much to ask. Wilt thou arise before daylight, and bear this letter from me to Pastor Nolan's lodgings? I would have done it myself, but mother has bidden me to come to her, and I may be detained until the time when Hota is to be hung; and the letter tells of matters pertaining to life and death. Seek out Pastor Nolan wherever he may be, and have speech of him after he has read the letter.'

'Cannot Nattee take it?' asked Lois.

'No!' Faith answered, fiercely. 'Why should she?'

But Lois did not reply. A quick suspicion darted through Faith's mind, sudden as lightning. It had never entered there before.

'Speak, Lois. I read thy thoughts. Thou wouldst fain not be the bearer of this letter?'

'I will take it,' said Lois, meekly. 'It concerns life and death, you say?'

'Yes!' said Faith, in quite a different tone of voice. But, after a pause of thought, she added: 'Then, as soon as the house is still, I will write what I have to say, and leave it here, on this chest; and thou wilt promise me to take it before the day is fully up, while there is yet time for action.'

'Yes! I promise,' said Lois. And Faith knew enough of her to feel sure that the deed would be done, however reluctantly.

The letter was written—laid on the chest; and, ere day dawned, Lois was astir, Faith watching her from between her half-closed eyelids—eyelids that had never been fully closed in sleep the livelong night. The instant Lois, cloaked and hooded, left the room, Faith sprang up, and prepared to go to her mother, whom she heard already stirring. Nearly every one in Salem was awake and up on this awful morning, though few were out of doors, as Lois passed along the streets. Here was the hastily erected gallows, the black shadow of which fell across the street with ghastly significance; now she had to pass the iron-barred gaol, through the unglazed windows of which she heard the fearful cry of a woman, and the sound of many footsteps. On she sped, sick almost to faintness, to the widow woman's where Mr. Nolan lodged. He was already up and abroad, gone, his hostess believed, to the gaol. Thither Lois, repeating the words 'for life and for death!' was forced to go. Retracing her steps, she was thankful to see him come out of those dismal portals, rendered more dismal for being in heavy shadow, just as she approached. What his errand had been she knew not; but he looked grave and sad, as she put Faith's letter into his hands, and stood before him quietly waiting, until he should read it, and deliver the expected answer. But, instead of opening it, he held it in his hand, apparently absorbed in thought. At last he spoke aloud, but more to himself than to her:

'My God! and is she then to die in this fearful delirium? It must be—can be—only delirium, that prompts such wild and horrible confessions. Mistress Barclay, I come from the presence of the Indian woman appointed to die. It seems, she considered herself betrayed last evening by her sentence not being respited, even after she had made confession of sin enough to bring down fire from heaven; and, it seems to me, the passionate, impotent anger of this helpless creature has turned to madness, for she appalls me by the additional revelations she has made to the keepers during the night—to me this morning. I could almost fancy that she thinks, by deepening the guilt she confesses, to escape this last dread punishment of all, as if, were a tithe of what she say true, one could suffer such a sinner to live. Yet to send her to death in such a state of mad terror! What is to be done?'

'Yet Scripture says that we are not to suffer witches in the land,' said Lois, slowly.

'True; I would but ask for a respite till the prayers of God's people had gone up for His mercy. Some would pray for her, poor wretch as she is. You would, Mistress Barclay, I am sure?' But he said it in a questioning tone.

'I have been praying for her in the night many a time,' said Lois, in a low voice. 'I pray for her in my heart at this moment; I suppose; they are bidden to put her out of the land, but I would not have her entirely God-forsaken. But, sir, you have not read my cousin's letter. And she bade me bring back an answer with much urgency.'

Still he delayed. He was thinking of the dreadful confession he came from hearing. If it were true, the beautiful earth was a polluted place, and he almost wished to die, to escape from such pollution, into the white innocence of those who stood in the presence of God.

Suddenly his eyes fell on Lois's pure, grave face, upturned and watching his. Faith in earthly goodness came over his soul in that instant, 'and he blessed her unaware.'

He put his hand on her shoulder, with an action half paternal—although the difference in their ages was not above a dozen years—and, bending a little towards her, whispered, half to himself, 'Mistress Barclay, you have done me good.'

'I!' said Lois, half affrighted—'I done you good! How?'

'By being what you are. But, perhaps, I should rather thank God, who sent you at the very moment when my soul was so disquieted.'

At this instant, they were aware of Faith standing in front of them, with a countenance of thunder. Her angry look made Lois feel guilty. She had not enough urged the pastor to read his letter, she thought; and it was indignation at this delay in what she had been commissioned to do with the urgency of life or death, that made her cousin lower at her so from beneath her straight black brows. Lois explained how she had not found Mr. Nolan at his lodgings, and had had to follow him to the door of the gaol. But Faith replied, with obdurate contempt:

'Spare thy breath, cousin Lois. It is easy seeing on what pleasant matters thou and the Pastor Nolan were talking. I marvel not at thy forgetfulness. My mind is changed. Give me back my letter, sir; it was about a poor matter—an old woman's life. And what is that compared to a young girl's love?'

Lois heard but for an instant; did not understand that her cousin, in her jealous anger, could suspect the existence of such a feeling as love between her and Mr. Nolan. No imagination as to its possibility had ever entered her mind; she had respected him, almost revered him—nay, had liked him as the probable husband of Faith. At the thought that her cousin could believe her guilty of such treachery, her grave eyes dilated, and fixed themselves on the flaming countenance of Faith. That serious, unprotesting manner of perfect innocence must have told on her accuser, had it not been that, at the same instant, the latter caught sight of the crimsoned and disturbed countenance of the pastor, who felt the veil rent off the unconscious secret of his heart. Faith snatched her letter out of his hands, and said:

'Let the witch hang! What care I? She has done harm enough with her charms and her sorcery on Pastor Tappau's girls. Let her die, and let all other witches look to themselves; for there be many kinds of witchcraft abroad. Cousin Lois, thou wilt like best to stop with Pastor Nolan, or I would pray thee to come back with me to breakfast.'

Lois was not to be daunted by jealous sarcasm. She held out her hand to Pastor Nolan, determined to take no heed of her cousin's mad words, but to bid him farewell in her accustomed manner. He hesitated before taking it, and when he did, it was with a convulsive squeeze that almost made her start. Faith waited and watched all, with set lips and vengeful eyes. She bade no farewell; she spake no word; but grasping Lois tightly by the back of the arm, she almost drove her before her down the street till they reached their home.

The arrangement for the morning was this: Grace Hickson and her son Manasseh were to be present at the hanging of the first witch executed in Salem, as pious and godly heads of a family. All the other members were strictly forbidden to stir out, until such time as the low-tolling bell announced that all was over in this world for Hota, the Indian witch. When the execution was ended, there was to be a solemn prayer-meeting of all the inhabitants of Salem; ministers had come from a distance to aid by the efficacy of their prayers in these efforts to purge the land of the devil and his servants. There was reason to think that the great old meeting-house would be crowded, and when Faith and Lois reached home, Grace Hickson was giving her directions to Prudence, urging her to be ready for an early start to that place. The stern old woman was troubled in her mind at the anticipation of the sight she was to see, before many minutes were over, and spoke in a more hurried and incoherent manner than was her wont. She was dressed in her Sunday best; but her face was very grey and colourless, and she seemed afraid to cease speaking about household affairs, for fear she should have time to think. Manasseh stood by her, perfectly, rigidly still; he also was in his Sunday clothes. His face, too, was paler than its wont, but it wore a kind of absent, rapt expression, almost like that of a man who sees a vision. As Faith entered, still holding Lois in her fierce grasp, Manasseh started and smiled; but still dreamily. His manner was so peculiar, that even his mother stayed her talking to observe him more closely; he was in that state of excitement which usually ended in what his mother and certain of her friends esteemed a prophetic revelation. He began to speak, at first very low, and then his voice increased in power:

'How beautiful is the land of Beulah, far over the sea, beyond the mountains! Thither the angels carry her, lying back in their arms like one fainting. They shall kiss away the black circle of death, and lay her down at the feet of the Lamb. I hear her pleading there for those on earth who consented to her death. O Lois! pray also for me, pray for me, miserable!'

When he uttered his cousin's name all their eyes turned towards her. It was to her that his vision related! She stood among them, amazed, awe-stricken, but not like one affrighted or dismayed. She was the first to speak:

'Dear friends, do not think of me; his words may or may not be true. I am in God's hands all the same, whether he have the gift of prophecy or not. Besides, hear you not that I end where all would fain end? Think of him, and of his needs. Such times as these always leave him exhausted and weary, when he comes out of them.'

And she busied herself in cares for his refreshment, aiding her aunt's trembling hands to set before him the requisite food, as he now sat tired and bewildered, gathering together with difficulty his scattered senses.

Prudence did all she could to assist and speed their departure. But Faith stood apart, watching in silence with her passionate, angry eyes.

As soon as they had set out on their solemn, fatal errand, Faith left the room. She had not tasted food or touched drink. Indeed, they all felt sick at heart. The moment her sister had gone up stairs, Prudence sprang to the settle on which Lois had thrown down her cloak and hood:

'Lend me your muffles and mantle, Cousin Lois. I never yet saw a woman hanged, and I see not why I should not go. I will stand on the edge of the crowd; no one will know me, and I will be home long before my mother.'

'No!' said Lois, 'that may not be. My aunt would be sore displeased. I wonder at you, Prudence, seeking to witness such a sight.' And as she spoke she held fast her cloak, which Prudence vehemently struggled for.

Faith returned, brought back possibly by the sound of the struggle. She smiled—a deadly smile.

'Give it up, Prudence. Strive no more with her. She has bought success in this world, and we are but her slaves.'

'Oh, Faith!' said Lois, relinquishing her hold of the cloak, and turning round with passionate reproach in her look and voice, 'what have I done that you should speak so of me; you, that have loved as I think one love a sister?'

Prudence did not lose her opportunity, but hastily arrayed herself in the mantle, which was too large for her, and which she had, therefore, considered as well adapted for concealment; but, as she went towards the door, her feet became entangled in the unusual length, and she fell, bruising her arm pretty sharply.

'Take care, another time, how you meddle with a witch's things,' said Faith, as one scarcely believing her own words, but at enmity with all the world in her bitter jealousy of heart. Prudence rubbed her arm and looked stealthily at Lois.

'Witch Lois! Witch Lois!' said she at last, softly, pulling a childish face of spite at her.

'Oh, hush, Prudence! Do not bandy such terrible words. Let me look at thine arm. I am sorry for thy hurt, only glad that it has kept thee from disobeying thy mother.'

'Away, away!' said Prudence, springing from her. 'I am afeard of her in very truth, Faith. Keep between me and the witch, or I will throw a stool at her.'

Faith smiled—it was a bad and wicked smile—but she did not stir to calm the fears she had called up in her young sister. Just at this moment, the bell began to toll. Hota, the Indian witch, was dead. Lois covered her face with her hands. Even Faith went a deadlier pale than she had been, and said, sighing, 'Poor Hota! But death is best.'

Prudence alone seemed unmoved by any thoughts connected with the solemn, monotonous sound. Her only consideration was, that now she might go out into the street and see the sights, and hear the news, and escape from the terror which she felt at the presence of her cousin. She flew up stairs to find her own mantle, ran down again, and past Lois, before the English girl had finished her prayer, and was speedily mingled among the crowd going to the meetinghouse. There also Faith and Lois came in due course of time, but separately, not together. Faith so evidently avoided Lois, that she, humbled and grieved, could not force her company upon her cousin, but loitered a little behind,—the quiet tears stealing down her face, shed for the many causes that had occurred this morning.

The meeting-house was full to suffocation; and, as it sometimes happens on such occasions, the greatest crowd was close about the doors, from the fact that few saw, on their first entrance, where there might be possible spaces into which they could wedge themselves. Yet they were impatient of any arrivals from the outside, and pushed and hustled Faith, and after her Lois, till the two were forced on to a conspicuous place in the very centre of the building, where there was no chance of a seat, but still space to stand in. Several stood around, the pulpit being in the middle, and already occupied by two ministers in Geneva bands and gowns, while other ministers, similarly attired, stood holding on to it, almost as if they were giving support instead of receiving it. Grace Hickson and her son sat decorously in their own pew, thereby showing that they had arrived early from the execution. You might almost have traced out the number of those who had been at the hanging of the Indian witch, by the expression of their countenances. They were awestricken into terrible repose; while the crowd pouring in, still pouring in, of those who had not attended the execution, looked all restless, and excited, and fierce. A buzz went round the meeting, that the stranger minister who stood along with Pastor Tappau in the pulpit was no other than Dr. Cotton Mather himself, come all the way from Boston to assist in purging Salem of witches.

And now Pastor Tappau began his prayer, extempore, as was the custom. His words were wild and incoherent, as might be expected from a man who had just been consenting to the bloody death of one who was, but a few days ago, a member of his own family; violent and passionate, as was to be looked for in the father of children, whom he believed to suffer so fearfully from the crime he would denounce before the Lord. He sat down at length from pure exhaustion. Then Dr. Cotton Mather stood forward: he did not utter more than a few words of prayer, calm in comparison with what had gone before, and then he went on to address the great crowd before him in a quiet, argumentative way, but arranging what he had to say with something of the same kind of skill which Antony used in his speech to the Romans after Cæsar's murder. Some of Dr. Mather's words have been preserved to us, as he afterwards wrote them down in one of his works. Speaking of those 'unbelieving Sadducees' who doubted the existence of such a crime, he said: 'Instead of their apish shouts and jeers at blessed Scripture, and histories which have such undoubted confirmation as that no man that has breeding enough to regard the common laws of human society will offer to doubt of them, it becomes us rather to adore the goodness of God, who from the mouths of babes and sucklings has ordained truth, and by the means of the sore-afflicted children of your godly pastor, has revealed the fact that the devils have with most horrid operations broken in upon your neighbourhood. Let us beseech Him that their power may be restrained, and that they go not so far in their evil machinations as they did but four years ago in the city of Boston, where I was the humble means, under God, of loosing from the power of Satan the four children of that religious and blessed man, Mr. Goodwin. These four babes of grace were bewitched by an Irish witch; there is no end to the narration of the torments they had to submit to. At one time they would bark like dogs, at another purr like cats; yea, they would fly like geese, and be carried with an incredible swiftness, having but just their toes now and then upon the ground, sometimes not once in twenty feet, and their arms waved like those of a bird. Yet at other times, by the hellish devices of the woman who had bewitched them, they could not stir without limping, for, by means of an invisible chain, she hampered their limbs, or, sometimes, by means of a noose, almost choked them. One in especial was subjected by this woman of Satan to such heat as of an oven, that I myself have seen the sweat drop from off her, while all around were moderately cold and well at ease. But not to trouble you with more of my stories, I will go on to prove that it was Satan himself that held power over her. For a very remarkable thing it was, that she was not permitted by that evil spirit to read any godly or religious book, speaking the truth as it is in Jesus. She could read Popish books well enough, while both sight and speech seemed to fail her when I gave her the Assembly's Catechism. Again, she was fond of that prelatical Book of Common Prayer, which is but the Roman mass-book in an English and ungodly shape. In the midst of her sufferings, if one put the Prayer-book into her hands it relieved her. Yet mark you, she could never be brought to read the Lord's Prayer, whatever book she met with it in, proving thereby distinctly that she was in league with the devil. I took her into my own house, that I, even as Dr. Martin Luther did, might wrestle with the devil and have my fling at him. But when I called my household to prayer, the devils that possessed her caused her to whistle, and sing, and yell in a discordant and hellish fashion.'

At this very instant, a shrill, clear whistle pierced all ears. Dr. Mather stopped for a moment:

'Satan is among you!' he cried. 'Look to yourselves!' And he prayed with fervour, as if against a present and threatening enemy; but no one heeded him. Whence came that ominous, unearthly whistle? Every man watched his neighbour. Again the whistle, out of their very midst! And then a bustle in a corner of the building, three or four people stirring, without any cause immediately perceptible to those at a distance, the movement spread, and, directly after, a passage even in that dense mass of people was cleared for two men, who bore forwards Prudence Hickson, lying rigid as a log of wood, in the convulsive position of one who suffered from an epileptic fit. They laid her down among the ministers who were gathered round the pulpit. Her mother came to her, sending up a wailing cry at the sight of her distorted child. Dr. Mather came down from the pulpit and stood over her, exorcising the devil in possession, as one accustomed to such scenes. The crowd pressed forward in mute horror. At length, her rigidity of form and feature gave way, and she was terribly convulsed—torn by the devil, as they called it. By-and-by the violence of the attack was over, and the spectators began to breathe once more, though still the former horror brooded over them, and they listened as if for the sudden ominous whistle again, and glanced fearfully around, as if Satan were at their backs picking out his next victim.

Meanwhile, Dr. Mather, Pastor Tappau, and one or two others were exhorting Prudence to reveal, if she could, the name of the person, the witch, who, by influence over Satan, had subjected the child to such torture as that which they had just witnessed. They bade her speak in the name of the Lord. She whispered a name in the low voice of exhaustion. None of the congregation could hear what it was. But the Pastor Tappau, when he heard it, drew back in dismay, while Dr. Mather, knowing not to whom the name belonged, cried out, in a clear, cold voice,

'Know ye one Lois Barclay; for it is she who hath bewitched this poor child?'

The answer was given rather by action than by word, although a low murmur went up from many. But all fell back, as far as falling back in such a crowd was possible, from Lois Barclay, where she stood,—and looked on her with surprise and horror. A space of some feet, where no possibility of space had seemed to be not a minute before, left Lois standing alone, with every eye fixed upon her in hatred and dread. She stood like one speechless, tongue-tied, as if in a dream. She a witch! accursed as witches were in the sight of God and man! Her smooth, healthy face became contracted into shrivel and pallor, but she uttered not a word, only looked at Dr. Mather with her dilated, terrified eyes.

Some one said, 'She is of the household of Grace Hickson, a God-fearing woman.' Lois did not know if the words were in her favour or not. She did not think about them, even; they told less on her than on any person present. She a witch! and the silver glittering Avon, and the drowning woman she had seen in her childhood at Barford,—at home in England,—were before her, and her eyes fell before her doom. There was some commotion—some rustling of papers; the magistrates of the town were drawing near the pulpit and consulting with the ministers. Dr. Mather spoke again:

'The Indian woman, who was hung this morning, named certain people, whom she deposed to having seen at the horrible meetings for the worship of Satan; but there is no name of Lois Barclay down upon the paper, although we are stricken at the sight of the names of some——'

An interruption—a consultation. Again Dr. Mather spoke:

'Bring the accused witch, Lois Barclay, near to this poor suffering child of Christ.'

They rushed forward to force Lois to the place where Prudence lay. But Lois walked forward of herself.

'Prudence,' she said, in such a sweet, touching voice, that, long afterwards, those who heard it that day, spoke of it to their children, 'have I ever said an unkind word to you, much less done you an ill turn? Speak, dear child. You did not know what you said just now, did you?'

But Prudence writhed away from her approach, and screamed out, as if stricken with fresh agony.

'Take her away! take her away! Witch Lois, witch Lois, who threw me down only this morning, and turned my arm black and blue.' And she bared her arm, as if in confirmation of her words. It was sorely bruised.

'I was not near you, Prudence!' said Lois, sadly. But that was only reckoned fresh evidence of her diabolical power.

Lois's brain began to get bewildered. Witch Lois! she a witch, abhorred of all men! Yet she would try to think, and make one more effort.

'Aunt Hickson,' she said, and Grace came forwards—'am I a witch, Aunt Hickson?' she asked; for her aunt, stern, harsh, unloving as she might be, was truth itself, and Lois thought—so near to delirium had she come—if her aunt condemned her, it was possible she might indeed be a witch.

Grace Hickson faced her unwillingly.

'It is a stain upon our family for ever,' was the thought in her mind.

'It is for God to judge whether thou art a witch, or not. Not for me.'

'Alas, alas!' moaned Lois; for she had looked at Faith, and learnt that no good word was to be expected from her gloomy face and averted eyes. The meeting-house was full of eager voices, repressed, out of reverence for the place, into tones of earnest murmuring that seemed to fill the air with gathering sounds of anger, and those who had at first fallen back from the place where Lois stood were now pressing forwards and round about her, ready to seize the young friendless girl, and bear her off to prison. Those who might have been, who ought to have been, her friends, were either averse or indifferent to her; though only Prudence made any open outcry upon her. That evil child cried out perpetually that Lois had cast a devilish spell upon her, and bade them keep the witch away from her; and, indeed, Prudence was strangely convulsed when once or twice Lois's perplexed and wistful eyes were turned in her direction. Here and there girls, women uttering strange cries, and apparently suffering from the same kind of convulsive fit as that which had attacked Prudence, were centres of a group of agitated friends, who muttered much and savagely of witchcraft, and the list which had been taken down only the night before from Hota's own lips. They demanded to have it made public, and objected to the slow forms of the law. Others, not so much or so immediately interested in the sufferers, were kneeling around, and praying aloud for themselves and their own safety, until the excitement should be so much quelled as to enable Dr. Cotton Mather to be again heard in prayer and exhortation.

And where was Manasseh? What said he? You must remember, that the stir of the outcry, the accusation, the appeals of the accused, all seemed to go on at once amid the buzz and din of the people who had come to worship God, but remained to judge and upbraid their fellow-creature. Till now Lois had only caught a glimpse of Manasseh, who was apparently trying to push forwards, but whom his mother was holding back with word and action, as Lois knew she would hold him back; for it was not for the first time that she was made aware how carefully her aunt had always shrouded his decent reputation among his fellow-citizens from the least suspicion of his seasons of excitement and incipient insanity. On such days, when he himself imagined that he heard prophetic voices, and saw prophetic visions, his mother would do much to prevent any besides his own family from seeing him; and now Lois, by a process swifter than reasoning, felt certain, from her one look at his face, when she saw it, colourless and deformed by intensity of expression, among a number of others all simply ruddy and angry, that he was in such a state that his mother would in vain do her utmost to prevent his making himself conspicuous. Whatever force or argument Grace used, it was of no avail. In another moment he was by Lois's side, stammering with excitement, and giving vague testimony, which would have been of little value in a calm court of justice, and was only oil to the smouldering fire of that audience.

'Away with her to gaol!' 'Seek out the witches!' 'The sin has spread into all households!' 'Satan is in the very midst of us!' 'Strike and spare not!' In vain Dr. Cotton Mather raised his voice in loud prayers, in which he assumed the guilt of the accused girl; no one listened, all were anxious to secure Lois, as if they feared she would vanish from before their very eyes; she, white, trembling, standing quite still in the tight grasp of strange, fierce men, her dilated eyes only wandering a little now and then in search of some pitiful face—some pitiful face that among all those hundreds was not to be found. While some fetched cords to bind her, and others, by low questions, suggested new accusations to the distempered brain of Prudence, Manasseh obtained a hearing once more. Addressing Dr. Cotton Mather, he said, evidently anxious to make clear some new argument that had just suggested itself to him: 'Sir, in this matter, be she witch or not, the end has been foreshown to me by the spirit of prophecy. Now, reverend sir, if the event be known to the spirit, it must have been foredoomed in the councils of God. If so, why punish her for doing that in which she had no free will?'

'Young man,' said Dr. Mather, bending down from the pulpit and looking very severely upon Manasseh, 'take care! you are trenching on blasphemy.'

'I do not care. I say it again. Either Lois Barclay is a witch, or she is not. If she is, it has been foredoomed for her, for I have seen a vision of her death as a condemned witch for many months past—and the voice has told me there was but one escape for her, Lois—the voice you know—' In his excitement he began to wander a little, but it was touching to see how conscious he was that by giving way he would lose the thread of the logical argument by which he hoped to prove that Lois ought not to be punished, and with what an effort he wrenched his imagination away from the old ideas, and strove to concentrate all his mind upon the plea that, if Lois was a witch, it had been shown him by prophecy; and if there was prophecy there must be foreknowledge; if foreknowledge, foredoom; if foredoom, no exercise of free will, and, therefore, that Lois was not justly amenable to punishment.

On he went, plunging into heresy, caring not—growing more and more passionate every instant, but directing his passion into keen argument, desperate sarcasm, instead of allowing it to excite his imagination. Even Dr. Mather felt himself on the point of being worsted in the very presence of this congregation, who, but a short half-hour ago, looked upon him as all but infallible. Keep a good heart, Cotton Mather! your opponent's eye begins to glare and flicker with a terrible yet uncertain light—his speech grows less coherent, and his arguments are mixed up with wild glimpses at wilder revelations made to himself alone. He has touched on the limits,—he has entered the borders of blasphemy, and with an awful cry of horror and reprobation the congregation rise up, as one man, against the blasphemer. Dr. Mather smiled a grim smile, and the people were ready to stone Manasseh, who went on, regardless, talking and raving.

'Stay, stay!' said Grace Hickson—all the decent family shame which prompted her to conceal the mysterious misfortune of her only son from public knowledge done away with by the sense of the immediate danger to his life. 'Touch him not. He knows not what he is saying. The fit is upon him. I tell you the truth before God. My son, my only son, is mad.'

They stood aghast at the intelligence. The grave young citizen, who had silently taken his part in life close by them in their daily lives—not mixing much with them, it was true, but looked up to, perhaps, all the more—the student of abstruse books on theology, fit to converse with the most learned ministers that ever came about those parts—was he the same with the man now pouring out wild words to Lois the witch, as if he and she were the only two present! A solution of it all occurred to them. He was another victim. Great was the power of Satan! Through the arts of the devil, that white statue of a girl had mastered the soul of Manasseh Hickson. So the word spread from mouth to mouth. And Grace heard it. It seemed a healing balsam for her shame. With wilful, dishonest blindness, she would not see—not even in her secret heart would she acknowledge, that Manasseh had been strange, and moody, and violent long before the English girl had reached Salem. She even found some specious reason for his attempt at suicide long ago. He was recovering from a fever—and though tolerably well in health, the delirium had not finally left him. But since Lois came, how headstrong he had been at times! how unreasonable! how moody! What a strange delusion was that which he was under, of being bidden by some voice to marry her! How he followed her about, and clung to her, as under some compulsion of affection! And over all reigned the idea that, if he were indeed suffering from being bewitched, he was not mad, and might again assume the honourable position he had held in the congregation and in the town, when the spell by which he was held was destroyed. So Grace yielded to the notion herself, and encouraged it in others, that Lois Barclay had bewitched both Manasseh and Prudence. And the consequence of this belief was, that Lois was to be tried, with little chance in her favour, to see whether she was a witch or no; and if a witch, whether she would confess, implicate others, repent, and live a life of bitter shame, avoided by all men, and cruelly treated by most; or die impenitent, hardened, denying her crime upon the gallows.

And so they dragged Lois away from the congregation of Christians to the gaol, to await her trial. I say 'dragged her,' because, although she was docile enough to have followed them whither they would, she was now so faint as to require extraneous force—poor Lois! who should have been carried and tended lovingly in her state of exhaustion, but, instead, was so detested by the multitude, who looked upon her as an accomplice of Satan in all his evil doings, that they cared no more how they treated her than a careless boy minds how he handles the toad that he is going to throw over the wall.

When Lois came to her full senses, she found herself lying on a short hard bed in a dark square room, which she at once knew must be a part of the city gaol. It was about eight feet square, it had stone walls on every side, and a grated opening high above her head, letting in all the light and air that could enter through about a square foot of aperture. It was so lonely, so dark to that poor girl, when she came slowly and painfully out of her long faint. She did so want human help in that struggle which always supervenes after a swoon; when the effort is to clutch at life, and the effort seems too much for the will. She did not at first understand where she was; did not understand how she came to be there, nor did she care to understand. Her physical instinct was to lie still and let the hurrying pulses have time to calm. So she shut her eyes once more. Slowly, slowly the recollection of the scene in the meeting-house shaped itself into a kind of picture before her. She saw within her eyelids, as it were, that sea of loathing faces all turned towards her, as towards something unclean and hateful. And you must remember, you who in the nineteenth century read this account, that witchcraft was a real terrible sin to her, Lois Barclay, two hundred years ago. The look on their faces, stamped on heart and brain, excited in her a sort of strange sympathy. Could it, oh God!— could it be true, that Satan had obtained the terrific power over her and her will, of which she had heard and read? Could she indeed be possessed by a demon and be indeed a witch, and yet till now have been unconscious of it? And her excited imagination recalled, with singular vividness, all she had ever heard on the subject—the horrible midnight sacrament, the very presence and power of Satan.

Then remembering every angry thought against her neighbour, against the impertinences of Prudence, against the overbearing authority of her aunt, against the persevering crazy suit of Manasseh, the indignation—only that morning, but such ages off in real time—at Faith's injustice; oh, could such evil thoughts have had devilish power given to them by the father of evil, and, all unconsciously to herself, have gone forth as active curses into the world? And so, on the ideas went careering wildly through the poor girl's brain—the girl thrown inward upon herself. At length, the sting of her imagination forced her to start up impatiently. What was this? A weight of iron on her legs—a weight stated afterwards, by the gaoler of Salem prison, to have been 'not more than eight pounds.' It was well for Lois it was a tangible ill, bringing her back from the wild illimitable desert in which her imagination was wandering. She took hold of the iron, and saw her torn stocking,—her bruised ankle, and began to cry pitifully, out of strange compassion with herself. They feared, then, that even in that cell she would find a way to escape. Why, the utter, ridiculous impossibility of the thing convinced her of her own innocence, and ignorance of all supernatural power; and the heavy iron brought her strangely round from the delusions that seemed to be gathering about her.

No! she never could fly out of that deep dungeon; there was no escape, natural or supernatural, for her, unless by man's mercy. And what was man's mercy in such times of panic? Lois knew that it was nothing; instinct more than reason taught her, that panic calls out cowardice, and cowardice cruelty. Yet she cried, cried freely, and for the first time, when she found herself ironed and chained. It seemed so cruel, so much as if her fellow-creatures had really learnt to hate and dread her—her, who had had a few angry thoughts, which God forgive! but whose thoughts had never gone into words, far less into actions. Why, even now she could love all the household at home, if they would but let her; yes, even yet, though she felt that it was the open accusation of Prudence and the withheld justifications of her aunt and Faith that had brought her to her present strait. Would they ever come and see her? Would kinder thoughts of her,—who had shared their daily bread for months and months,—bring them to see her, and ask her whether it were really she who had brought on the illness of Prudence, the derangement of Manasseh's mind?

No one came. Bread and water were pushed in by some one, who hastily locked and unlocked the door, and cared not to see if he put them within his prisoner's reach, or perhaps thought that physical fact mattered little to a witch. It was long before Lois could reach them; and she had something of the natural hunger of youth left in her still, which prompted her, lying her length on the floor, to weary herself with efforts to obtain the bread. After she had eaten some of it, the day began to wane, and she thought she would lay her down and try to sleep. But before she did so, the gaoler heard her singing the Evening Hymn:

Glory   to   thee,   my   God,   this   night,
For all the blessings of the light.

And a dull thought came into his dull mind, that she was thankful for few blessings, if she could tune up her voice to sing praises after this day of what, if she were a witch, was shameful detection in abominable practices, and if not—. Well, his mind stopped short at this point in his wondering contemplation. Lois knelt down and said the Lord's Prayer, pausing just a little before one clause, that she might be sure that in her heart of hearts she did forgive. Then she looked at her ankle, and the tears came into her eyes once again, but not so much because she was hurt, as because men must have hated her so bitterly before they could have treated her thus. Then she lay down, and fell asleep.

The next day, she was led before Mr. Hathorn and Mr. Curwin, justices of Salem, to be accused legally and publicly of witchcraft. Others were with her, under the same charge. And when the prisoners were brought in, they were cried out at by the abhorrent crowd. The two Tappaus, Prudence, and one or two other girls of the same age were there, in the character of victims of the spells of the accused. The prisoners were placed about seven or eight feet from the justices and the accusers between the justices and them; the former were then ordered to stand right before the justices. All this Lois did at their bidding, with something of the wondering docility of a child, but not with any hope of softening the hard, stony look of detestation that was on all the countenances around her, save those that were distorted by more passionate anger. Then an officer was bidden to hold each of her hands, and Justice Hathorn bade her keep her eyes continually fixed on him, for this reason—which, however, was not told to her—lest, if she looked on Prudence, the girl might either fall into a fit, or cry out that she was suddenly and violently hurt. If any heart could have been touched of that cruel multitude, they would have felt some compassion for the sweet young face of the English girl, trying so meekly to do all that she was ordered, her face quite white, yet so full of sad gentleness, her grey eyes, a little dilated by the very solemnity of her position, fixed with the intent look of innocent maidenhood on the stern face of Justice Hathorn. And thus they stood in silence, one breathless minute. Then they were bidden to say the Lord's Prayer. Lois went through it as if alone in her cell; but, as she had done alone in her cell the night before, she made a little pause, before the prayer to be forgiven as she forgave. And at this instant of hesitation—as if they had been on the watch for it—they all cried out upon her for a witch, and when the clamour ended the justices bade Prudence Hickson come forwards. Then Lois turned a little to one side, wishing to see at least one familiar face; but when her eyes fell upon Prudence, the girl stood stock-still, and answered no questions, nor spoke a word, and the justices declared that she was struck dumb by witchcraft. Then some behind took Prudence under the arms, and would have forced her forwards to touch Lois, possibly esteeming that as a cure for her being bewitched. But Prudence had hardly been made to take three steps before she struggled out of their arms, and fell down writhing as in a fit, calling out with shrieks, and entreating Lois to help her, and save her from her torment. Then all the girls began 'to tumble down like swine' (to use the words of an eye-witness) and to cry out upon Lois and her fellow-prisoners. These last were now ordered to stand with their hands stretched out, it being imagined that if the bodies of the witches were arranged in the form of a cross they would lose their evil power. By-and-by Lois felt her strength going, from the unwonted fatigue of such a position, which she had borne patiently until the pain and weariness had forced both tears and sweat down her face, and she asked in a low, plaintive voice, if she might not rest her head for a few moments against the wooden partition. But Justice Hathorn told her she had strength enough to torment others, and should have strength enough to stand. She sighed a little, and bore on, the clamour against her and the other accused increasing every moment; the only way she could keep herself from utterly losing consciousness was by distracting herself from present pain and danger, and saying to herself verses of the Psalms as she could remember them, expressive of trust in God. At length she was ordered back to gaol, and dimly understood that she and others were sentenced to be hanged for witchcraft. Many people now looked eagerly at Lois, to see if she would weep at this doom. If she had had strength to cry, it might—it was just possible that it might—have been considered a plea in her favour, for witches could not shed tears, but she was too exhausted and dead. All she wanted was to lie down once more on her prison-bed, out of the reach of men's cries of abhorrence, and out of shot of their cruel eyes. So they led her back to prison, speechless and tearless.

But rest gave her back her power of thought and suffering. Was it, indeed, true that she was to die? She, Lois Barclay, only eighteen, so well, so young, so full of love and hope as she had been, till but these little days past! What would they think of it at home—real, dear home at Barford, in England? There they had loved her; there she had gone about, singing and rejoicing all the day long in the pleasant meadows by the Avon side. Oh, why did father and mother die, and leave her their bidding to come here to this cruel New England shore, where no one had wanted her, no one had cared for her, and where now they were going to put her to a shameful death as a witch? And there would be no one to send kindly messages by to those she should never see more. Never more! Young Lucy was living, and joyful—probably thinking of her, and of his declared intention of coming to fetch her home to be his wife this very spring. Possibly he had forgotten her; no one knew. A week before, she would have been indignant at her own distrust in thinking for a minute that he could forget. Now, she doubted all men's goodness for a time; for those around her were deadly, and cruel, and relentless.

Then she turned round, and beat herself with angry blows (to speak in images), for ever doubting her lover. Oh! if she were but with him! Oh! if she might but be with him! He would not let her die; but would hide her in his bosom from the wrath of this people, and carry her back to the old home at Barford. And he might even now be sailing on the wide blue sea, coming nearer, nearer every moment, and yet be too late after all.

So the thoughts chased each other through her head all that feverish night, till she clung almost deliriously to life, and wildly prayed that she might not die; at least, not just yet, and she so young!

Pastor Tappau and certain elders roused her up from a heavy sleep, late on the morning of the following day. All night long she had trembled and cried, till morning had come peering in through the square grating up above. It soothed her, and she fell asleep, to be awakened, as I have said, by Pastor Tappau.

'Arise!' said he, scrupling to touch her, from his superstitious idea of her evil powers. 'It is noonday.'

'Where am I?' said she, bewildered at this unusual wakening, and the array of severe faces all gazing upon her with reprobation.

'You are in Salem gaol, condemned for a witch.'

'Alas! I had forgotten for an instant,' said she, dropping her head upon her breast.

'She has been out on a devilish ride all night long, doubtless, and is weary and perplexed this morning,' whispered one, in so low a voice that he did not think she could hear; but she lifted up her eyes, and looked at him, with mute reproach.

'We are come' said Pastor Tappau, 'to exhort you to confess your great and manifold sin.'

'My great and manifold sin!' repeated Lois to herself, shaking her head.

'Yea, your sin of witchcraft. If you will confess, there may yet be balm in Gilead.'

One of the elders, struck with pity at the young girl's wan, shrunken look, said, that if she confessed, and repented, and did penance, possibly her life might yet be spared.

A sudden flash of light came into her sunk, dulled eye. Might she yet live? Was it yet in her power?

Why, no one knew how soon Ralph Lucy might be here, to take her away for ever into the peace of a new home! Life! Oh, then, all hope was not over—perhaps she might still live, and not die. Yet the truth came once more out of her lips, almost without any exercise of her will.

'I am not a witch,' she said.

Then Pastor Tappau blindfolded her, all unresisting, but with languid wonder in her heart as to what was to come next. She heard people enter the dungeon softly, and heard whispering voices; then her hands were lifted up and made to touch some one near, and in an instant she heard a noise of struggling, and the well-known voice of Prudence shrieking out in one of her hysterical fits, and screaming to be taken away and out of that place. It seemed to Lois as if some of her judges must have doubted of her guilt, and demanded yet another test. She sat down heavily on her bed, thinking she must be in a horrible dream, so compassed about with dangers and enemies did she seem. Those in the dungeon—and by the oppression of the air she perceived that they were many—kept on eager talking in low voices. She did not try to make out the sense of the fragments of sentences that reached her dulled brain, till, all at once, a word or two made her understand they were discussing the desirableness of applying the whip or the torture to make her confess, and reveal by what means the spell she had cast upon those whom she had bewitched could be dissolved. A thrill of affright ran through her; and she cried out, beseechingly:

'I beg you, sirs, for God's mercy sake, that you do not use such awful means. I may say anything—nay, I may accuse any one if I am subjected to such torment as I have heard tell about. For I am but a young girl, and not very brave, or very good, as some are.'

It touched the hearts of one or two to see her standing there; the tears streaming down from below the coarse handkerchief tightly bound over her eyes; the clanking chain fastening the heavy weight to the slight ankle; the two hands held together as if to keep down a convulsive motion.

'Look!' said one of these. 'She is weeping. They say no witch can weep tears.'

But another scoffed at this test, and bade the first remember how those of her own family, the Hicksons even, bore witness against her.

Once more she was bidden to confess. The charges, esteemed by all men (as they said) to have been proven against her, were read over to her, with all the testimony borne against her in proof thereof. They told her that, considering the godly family to which she belonged, it had been decided by the magistrates and ministers of Salem that he should have her life spared, if she would own her guilt, make reparation, and submit to penance; but that if not, she, and others convicted of witchcraft along with her, were to be hung in Salem market-place on the next Thursday morning (Thursday being market day). And when they had thus spoken, they waited silently for her answer. It was a minute or two before she spoke. She had sat down again upon the bed meanwhile, for indeed she was very weak. She asked, 'May I have this handkerchief unbound from my eyes, for indeed, sirs, it hurts me?'

The occasion for which she was blindfolded being over, the bandage was taken off, and she was allowed to see. She looked pitifully at the stern faces around her, in grim suspense as to what her answer would be. Then she spoke:

'Sirs, I must choose death with a quiet conscience, rather than life to be gained by a lie. I am not a witch. I know not hardly what you mean when you say I am. I have done many, many things very wrong in my life; but I think God will forgive me them for my Saviour's sake.'

'Take not His name on your wicked lips,' said Pastor Tappau, enraged at her resolution of not confessing, and scarcely able to keep himself from striking her. She saw the desire he had, and shrank away in timid fear. Then Justice Hathorn solemnly read the legal condemnation of Lois Barclay to death by hanging, as a convicted witch. She murmured something which nobody heard fully, but which sounded like a prayer for pity and compassion on her tender years and friendless estate. Then they left her to all the horrors of that solitary, loathsome dungeon, and the strange terror of approaching death.

Outside the prison walls, the dread of the witches, and the excitement against witchcraft, grew with fearful rapidity. Numbers of women, and men, too, were accused, no matter what their station of life and their former character had been. On the other side, it is alleged that upwards of fifty persons were grievously vexed by the devil, and those to whom he had imparted of his power for vile and wicked considerations. How much of malice, distinct, unmistakable personal malice, was mixed up with these accusations, no one can now tell. The dire statistics of this time tell us, that fifty-five escaped death by confessing themselves guilty, one hundred and fifty were in prison, more than two hundred accused, and upwards of twenty suffered death, among whom was the minister I have called Nolan, who was traditionally esteemed to have suffered through hatred of his co-pastor. One old man, scorning the accusation, and refusing to plead at his trial, was, according to the law, pressed to death for his contumacy. Nay, even dogs were accused of witchcraft, suffered the legal penalties, and are recorded among the subjects of capital punishment. One young man found means to effect his mother's escape from confinement, fled with her on horseback, and secreted her in the Blueberry Swamp, not far from Taplay's Brook, in the Great Pasture; he concealed her here in a wigwam which he built for her shelter, provided her with food and clothing, and comforted and sustained her until after the delusion had passed away. The poor creature must, however, have suffered dreadfully, for one of her arms was fractured in the all but desperate effort of getting her out of prison.

But there was no one to try and save Lois. Grace Hickson would fain have ignored her altogether. Such a taint did witchcraft bring upon a whole family, that generations of blameless life were not at that day esteemed sufficient to wash it out. Besides, you must remember that Grace, along with most people of her time, believed most firmly in the reality of the crime of witchcraft. Poor, forsaken Lois, believed in it herself, and it added to her terror, for the gaoler, in an unusually communicative mood, told her that nearly every cell was now full of witches; and it was possible he might have to put one, if more came, in with her. Lois knew that she was no witch herself; but not the less did she believe that the crime was abroad, and largely shared in by evil-minded persons who had chosen to give up their souls to Satan; and she shuddered with terror at what the gaoler said, and would have asked him to spare her this companionship if it were possible. But, somehow, her senses were leaving her, and she could not remember the right words in which to form her request, until he had left the place.

The only person who yearned after Lois—who would have befriended her if he could—was Manasseh: poor, mad Manasseh. But he was so wild and outrageous in his talk, that it was all his mother could do to keep his state concealed from public observation. She had for this purpose given him a sleeping potion; and, while he lay heavy and inert under the influence of the poppy-tea, his mother bound him with cords to the ponderous, antique bed in which he slept. She looked broken-hearted while she did this office, and thus acknowledged the degradation of her first-born—him of whom she had ever been so proud.

Late that evening, Grace Hickson stood in Lois's cell, hooded and cloaked up to her eyes. Lois was sitting quite still, playing idly with a bit of string which one of the magistrates had dropped out of his pocket that morning. Her aunt was standing by her for an instant or two in silence, before Lois seemed aware of her presence. Suddenly she looked up, and uttered a little cry, shrinking away from the dark figure. Then, as if her cry had loosened Grace's tongue, she began:

'Lois Barclay, did I ever do you any harm?' Grace did not know how often her want of loving-kindness had pierced the tender heart of the stranger under her roof; nor did Lois remember it against her now. Instead, Lois's memory was filled with grateful thoughts of how much that might have been left undone, by a less conscientious person, her aunt had done for her, and she half stretched out her arms as to a friend in that desolate place, while she answered:

'Oh no, no you were very good! very kind!'

But Grace stood immovable.

'I did you no harm, although I never rightly knew why you came to us.'

'I was sent by my mother on her death-bed,' moaned Lois, covering her face. It grew darker every instant. Her aunt stood, still and silent.

'Did any of mine ever wrong you?' she asked, after a time.

'No, no; never, till Prudence said—Oh, aunt, do you think I am a witch?' And now Lois was standing up, holding by Grace's cloak, and trying to read her face. Grace drew herself, ever so little, away from the girl, whom she dreaded, and yet sought to propitiate.

'Wiser than I, godlier than I, have said it. But oh, Lois, Lois! he was my first-born. Loose him from the demon, for the sake of Him whose name I dare not name in this terrible building, filled with them who have renounced the hopes of their baptism; loose Manasseh from his awful state, if ever I or mine did you a kindness!'

'You ask me for Christ's sake,' said Lois. 'I can name that holy name—for oh, aunt! indeed, and in holy truth, I am no witch; and yet I am to die—to be hanged! Aunt, do not let them kill me! I am so young, and I never did any one any harm that I know of.'

'Hush! for very shame! This afternoon I have bound my first-born with strong cords, to keep him from doing himself or us a mischief—he is so frenzied. Lois Barclay, look here!' and Grace knelt down at her niece's feet, and joined her hands as if in prayer—'I am a proud woman, God forgive me! and I never thought to kneel to any save to Him. And now I kneel at your feet, to pray you to release my children, more especially my son Manasseh, from the spells you have put upon them. Lois, hearken to me, and I will pray to the Almighty for you, if yet there may be mercy.'

'I cannot do it; I never did you or yours any wrong. How can I undo it? How can I?' And she wrung her hands in intensity of conviction of the inutility of aught she could do.

Here Grace got up, slowly, stiffly, and sternly. She stood aloof from the chained girl, in the remote corner of the prison cell near the door, ready to make her escape as soon as she had cursed the witch, who would not, or could not, undo the evil she had wrought. Grace lifted up her right hand, and held it up on high, as she doomed Lois to be accursed for ever, for her deadly sin, and her want of mercy even at this final hour. And, lastly, she summoned her to meet her at the judgment-seat, and answer for this deadly injury done to both souls and bodies of those who had taken her in, and received her when she came to them an orphan and a stranger.

Until this last summons, Lois had stood as one who hears her sentence and can say nothing against it, for she knows all would be in vain. But she raised her head when she heard her aunt speak of the judgment-seat, and at the end of Grace's speech she, too, lifted up her right hand, as if solemnly pledging herself by that action, and replied:

'Aunt! I will meet you there. And there you will know my innocence of this deadly thing. God have mercy on you and yours!'

Her calm voice maddened Grace, and making a gesture as if she plucked up a handful of dust of the floor, and threw it at Lois, she cried:

'Witch! witch! ask mercy for thyself—I need not your prayers. Witches' prayers are read backwards. I spit at thee, and defy thee!' And so she went away.

Lois sat moaning that whole night through. 'God comfort me! God strengthen me!' was all she could remember to say. She just felt that want, nothing more,—all other fears and wants seemed dead within her. And when the gaoler brought in her breakfast the next morning, he reported her as 'gone silly;' for, indeed, she did not seem to know him, but kept rocking herself to and fro, and whispering softly to herself, smiling a little from time to time.

But God did comfort her, and strengthen her too late on that Wednesday afternoon, they thrust another 'witch' into her cell, bidding the two, with opprobrious words, keep company together. The new comer fell prostrate with the push given her from without; and Lois, not recognizing anything but an old ragged woman lying helpless on her face on the ground, lifted her up; and lo! it was Nattee—dirty, filthy indeed, mud-pelted, stone-bruised, beaten, and all astray in her wits with the treatment she had received from the mob outside. Lois held her in her arms, and softly wiped the old brown wrinkled face with her apron, crying over it, as she had hardly yet cried over her own sorrows. For hours she tended the old Indian woman—tended her bodily woes; and as the poor scattered senses of the savage creature came slowly back, Lois gathered her infinite dread of the morrow, when she too, as well as Lois, was to be led out to die, in face of all that infuriated crowd. Lois sought in her own mind for some source of comfort for the old woman, who shook like one in the shaking palsy at the dread of death—and such a death.

When all was quiet through the prison, in the deep dead midnight, the gaoler outside the door heard Lois telling, as if to a young child, the marvellous and sorrowful story of one who died on the cross for us and for our sakes. As long as she spoke, the Indian woman's terror seemed lulled; but the instant she paused, for weariness, Nattee cried out afresh, as if some wild beast were following her close through the dense forests in which she had dwelt in her youth. And then Lois went on, saying all the blessed words she could remember, and comforting the helpless Indian woman with the sense of the presence of a Heavenly Friend. And in comforting her, Lois was comforted; in strengthening her, Lois was strengthened.

The morning came, and the summons to come forth and die came. They who entered the cell found Lois asleep, her face resting on the slumbering old woman, whose head she still held in her lap. She did not seem clearly to recognize where she was, when she awakened; the 'silly' look had returned to her wan face; all she appeared to know was, that somehow or another, through some peril or another, she had to protect the poor Indian woman. She smiled faintly when she saw the bright light of the April day; and put her arm round Nattee, and tried to keep the Indian quiet with hushing, soothing words of broken meaning, and holy fragments of the Psalms. Nattee tightened her hold upon Lois as they drew near the gallows, and the outrageous crowd below began to hoot and yell. Lois redoubled her efforts to calm and encourage Nattee, apparently unconscious that any of the opprobrium, the hootings, the stones, the mud, was directed towards her herself. But when they took Nattee from her arms, and led her out to suffer first, Lois seemed all at once to recover her sense of the present terror. She gazed wildly around, stretched out her arms as if to some person in the distance, who was yet visible to her, and cried out once with a voice that thrilled through all who heard it, 'Mother!' Directly afterwards, the body of Lois the Witch swung in the air, and every one stood, with hushed breath, with a sudden wonder, like a fear of deadly crime, fallen upon them.

The stillness and the silence were broken by one crazed and mad, who came rushing up the steps of the ladder, and caught Lois's body in his arms, and kissed her lips with wild passion. And then, as if it were true what the people believed, that he was possessed by a demon, he sprang down, and rushed through the crowd, out of the bounds of the city, and into the dark dense forest, and Manasseh Hickson was no more seen of Christian man.

The people of Salem had awakened from their frightful delusion before the autumn, when Captain Holdernesse and Ralph Lucy came to find out Lois, and bring her home to peaceful Barford, in the pleasant country of England. Instead, they led them to the grassy grave where she lay at rest, done to death by mistaken men. Ralph Lucy shook the dust off his feet in quitting Salem, with a heavy, heavy heart; and lived a bachelor all his life long for her sake.

Long years afterwards, Captain Holdernesse sought him out, to tell him some news that he thought might interest the grave miller of the Avonside. Captain Holdernesse told him that in the previous year, it was then 1713, the sentence of excommunication against the witches of Salem was ordered, in godly sacramental meeting of the church, to be erased and blotted out, and that those who met together for this purpose 'humbly requested the merciful God would pardon whatsoever sin, error, or mistake was in the application of justice, through our merciful High Priest, who knoweth how to have compassion on the ignorant, and those that are out of the way.' He also said that Prudence Hickson—now woman grown—had made a most touching and pungent declaration of sorrow and repentance before the whole church, for the false and mistaken testimony she had given in several instances, among which she particularly mentioned that of her cousin Lois Barclay. To all which Ralph Lucy only answered:

'No repentance of theirs can bring her back to life.'

Then Captain Holdernesse took out a paper, and read the following humble and solemn declaration of regret on the part of those who signed it, among whom Grace Hickson was one:

'We, whose names are undersigned, being, in the year 1692, called to serve as jurors in court of Salem, on trial of many who were by some suspected guilty of doing acts of witchcraft upon the bodies of sundry persons; we confess that we ourselves were not capable to understand, nor able to withstand, the mysterious delusions of the powers of darkness, and prince of the air, but were, for want of knowledge in ourselves, and better information from others, prevailed with to take up with such evidence against the accused, as, on further consideration, and better information, we justly fear was insufficient for the touching the lives of any (Deut. xvii. 6), whereby we fear we have been instrumental, with others, though ignorantly and unwittingly, to bring upon ourselves and this people of the Lord the guilt of innocent blood; which sin, the Lord saith in Scripture, he would not pardon (2 Kings, xxiv. 4), that is, we suppose, in regard of his temporal judgments. We do, therefore, signify to all in general (and to the surviving sufferers in special) our deep sense of, and sorrow for, our errors, in acting on such evidence to the condemning of any person; and do hereby declare, that we justly fear that we were sadly deluded and mistaken, for which we are much disquieted and distressed in our minds, and do therefore humbly beg forgiveness, first of God for Christ's sake, for this our error; and pray that God would not impute the guilt of it to ourselves nor others; and we also pray that we may be considered candidly and aright by the living sufferers, as being then under the power of a strong and general delusion, utterly unacquainted with, and not experienced in, matters of that nature.

'We do heartily ask forgiveness of you all, whom we have justly offended; and do declare, according to our present minds, we would none of us do such things again on such grounds for the whole world; praying you to accept of this in way of satisfaction for our offence, and that you would bless the inheritance of the Lord, that he may be entreated for the land.

'FOREMAN, THOMAS FISK, &c.'

To the reading of this paper Ralph Lucy made no reply save this, even more gloomily than before:

'All their repentance will avail nothing to my Lois, nor will it bring back her life.'

Then Captain Holdernesse spoke once more, and said that on the day of the general fast, appointed to be held all through New England, when the meeting-houses were crowded, an old, old man with white hair had stood up in the place in which he was accustomed to worship, and had handed up into the pulpit a written confession, which he had once or twice essayed to read for himself, acknowledging his great and grievous error in the matter of the witches of Salem, and praying for the forgiveness of God and of his people, ending with an entreaty that all then present would join with him in prayer that his past conduct might not bring down the displeasure of the Most High upon his country, his family, or himself. That old man, who was no other than Justice Sewall, remained standing all the time that his confession was read; and at the end he said, 'The good and gracious God be pleased to save New England and me and my family.' And then it came out that, for years past, Judge Sewall had set apart a day for humiliation and prayer, to keep fresh in his mind a sense of repentance and sorrow for the part he had borne in these trials, and that this solemn anniversary he was pledged to keep as long as he lived, to show his feeling of deep humiliation.

Ralph Lucy's voice trembled as he spoke:

'All this will not bring my Lois to life again, or give me back the hope of my youth.'

But—as Captain Holdernesse shook his head (for what word could he say, or how dispute what was so evidently true?)—Ralph added, 'What is the day, know you, that this justice has set apart?'

'The twenty-ninth of April.'

'Then on that day will I, here at Barford in England, join my prayer as long as I live with the repentant judge, that his sin may be blotted out and no more had in remembrance. She would have willed it so.'

The Witch in the Well

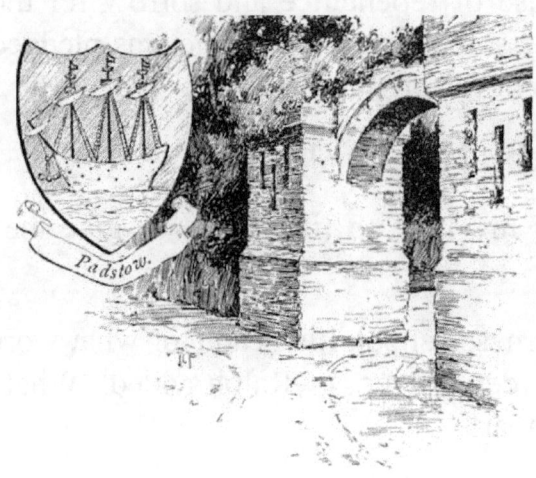

Padstow

Once upon a time seven little maids of Padstow Town met together in Beck Lane to play a game called 'The Witch in the Well.' As they stood waiting for the child who was to act the witch, an old woman dressed in a steeple-hat and chintz petticoat came down the lane towards them.

'What are you doing here, my pretty maids?' she asked.

'Waiting for our witch,' answered the children, wondering who this strange-looking, oddly-dressed old woman could be. 'We are going to play "Witch in the Well."'

'Are you?' said the queer old body. 'I used to play that nice game when I was young like you, and should love to play it once again before I die. The little maid who was to have been your witch tumbled down on the cobble-stones in the market-place and hurt herself as she was coming hither,' she added, as they stared at her in amazement, 'and won't be able to play with you to-day. Will you let *me* be your witch instead of your little friend?'

'If you like, ma'am,' answered one of the children, after a hasty glance at her companions for consent.

'Thank you,' cried the old woman. 'It will be the most exciting game you ever played in all your life;' and, lifting her petticoats as if to display her high-heeled shoes and red stockings, she hobbled across the road to a well under a Gothic arch.

When the old crone had taken her seat inside the ancient well—and which was called the Witch's Well—Betty, the child who was to play the Mother in the game, took the other six little maids to a tumble-down cottage opposite the well, and the game began.

The Little Mother told her children—who were called after the six working days of the week—that she was going down to Padstow Town to sell her eggs, and that they must not leave the cottage, as the Witch o' the Well was about.

'Mind the old witch doesn't come and carry you away,' the wee maids said one to another when the Little Mother had gone.

As they were saying this, the old woman in the chintz petticoat and steeple-hat came to the door, and looked over the hatch.

'May I come in and light my pipe?' she asked.

'Iss, ma'am,' said Tuesday, unfastening the hatch; and when the old crone had come in and lighted her pipe, she crooked her lean old arm round Monday and took her away.

'Where is Monday?' asked the Little Mother when she had come back to her cottage, quick to see that one of her children was gone.

'An old woman came to light her pipe and took her away,' said Tuesday.

'It was the old Witch o' the Well,' cried the Little Mother. 'I'll go and see what she has done with her.'

And across the road to the well she went, and, stooping down and looking in, she saw an old woman sitting in the back of the well smoking a pipe.

'Where is my little maid Monday?' she demanded sternly.

'I gave her a piece of thunder-and-lightning[1] and sent her to Chapel Stile to see if the waves were breaking on the Doombar,' answered the witch, knocking the ashes out of her pipe.

'I am off to Chapel Stile to look for Monday,' said the Little Mother, returning to the cottage. 'Be sure you don't let the old witch come in whilst I am away.'

Betty's back was no sooner turned than the same old woman came to the door.

'May I come in and light my pipe?' she asked.

'Iss, if you please, ma'am,' said Tuesday, forgetting her mother's injunction.

The old crone came in, lighted her pipe, and took away Tuesday!

'Mind the old Witch o' the Well don't come and take you away like she did Monday and Tuesday,' the children were saying to each other when Betty came back from her fruitless search for Monday.

'What! has the bad old witch come and taken away Tuesday?' cried the Little Mother. 'Dear! what ever *shall* I do now? I can't find Monday, and now my poor little Tuesday is gone!'

She rushed across the road to the well where the old witch was sitting, as before, calmly smoking her pipe.

'What have you done with Tuesday?' she demanded.

'I gave her a piece of saffron cake and sent her out to Lelizzick to ask Farmer Chapman to sell me a bag of sheep's wool for spinning,' the witch made answer.

'I am going out to Lelizzick to look for Tuesday,' said the Little Mother, rushing back to her children. 'Be sure you don't let the old witch come in. If you do, she will take you all away, and then what shall I do without my dear little maids?'

Betty was scarcely out of sight when a steeple-hat was seen at the window, and a pair of eerie eyes looked in.

Before the children could shut the door and its hatch, the old witch had come into the cottage.

'A puff of wind blew out my pipe,' she said. 'May I light it with a twig from your fire?'

'Iss,' answered Wednesday somewhat doubtfully. 'But Mother told us we were not to let you come in, because, if we did, you would take us away as you did Monday and Tuesday.'

'Did she?' cackled the witch, taking a bit of stick from the fire and thrusting it into her pipe. 'Well, I only want one of you now,' and looking round the room, her glance fell on Wednesday, and crooking her arm round her, she carried her off to the well.

'I have been out to Lelizzick and can't find Tuesday,' cried the Little Mother, coming into the cottage as the witch, with Wednesday under her arm, disappeared into the well. 'Oh! where is Wednesday?' looking round the room and seeing *another* of her children missing.

'The old witch came in before we could shut the door, and took our little sister away,' said the children.

'This is wisht news, sure 'nough,' wailed the Little Mother, and off she rushed to the well, where the witch was sitting smoking.

'What have you been and done with Wednesday?' she asked angrily.

'I gave her a bit of figgy-pudding, and sent her to Place House to ask if Squire Prideaux's housekeeper would kindly give an old body a bottle of their good physic to cure her rheumatics.'

'I'm going up to Place House to see if Wednesday is there,' said the Little Mother, looking in at the window of the cottage. 'If the witch should come to the door whilst I am away, don't let her come in, whatever you do!'

When she had gone to Place House, an old mansion standing above Padstow Town, the old witch left the well, and before the children saw her, she had pushed open the door, and stood in the doorway, looking in.

'May I come in and light my pipe?' she asked.

'No,' answered Thursday.

But she came in, nevertheless, and having lighted her pipe, she caught up Thursday and took her across to the well.

'What! has the witch been here again, and taken away Thursday?' exclaimed the Little Mother when she came back from Place House without finding Wednesday, discovering that another of her children was gone.

'Iss,' sighed Friday. 'She came over the doorsill before we saw her.'

'This is too dreadful!' cried the poor Little Mother. 'I shall soon have no little maids left to call my own!' and wringing her hands, she went across the lane to the well.

'What have you been and done with Thursday, you bad old witch?' she demanded.

'I gave her a piece of limpet-pie, and sent her to London Churchtown to buy me a steeple-hat and a broom,' the witch made answer, rudely puffing her pipe in Betty's face. 'If you go there in Marrowbone Stage[2], you will perhaps find her.'

'I am off to London Churchtown in Marrowbone Stage to look for Thursday,' cried the Little Mother, returning to her cottage in great haste and excitement. 'Keep the door and hatch locked and barred till I come back, and then, if you are good children and do as I bid, I will bring you home each a gold ring.'

When the Little Mother had driven away in Marrowbone Stage to London Churchtown in search of Thursday, Friday saw the witch leave the well and cross the road to their cottage.

'Shut the door quickly and bar it,' she cried to Little Saturday.

And Saturday had but slipped the bolt into its socket when the old hag was at the door, knocking loudly to be let in.

'My pipe has gone out again,' she shrilled through the keyhole. 'May I come in and light it?'

'*No!*' answered Friday. 'Mother said you would take us away as you did poor Monday, Tuesday, Wednesday, and Thursday, if we let you in.'

'I must come in and light my pipe,' insisted the witch. 'And if you don't open the door, I'll come through the keyhole;' and as the children would not open the door, through the keyhole she came!

Having lighted her pipe and unbolted the door, she caught up both children and carried them away, and when the tired Little Mother returned from London Churchtown in a fruitless search for Thursday, she found to her dismay not only Friday gone, but dear Little Saturday!

She hurried to the well in an agony of despair.

'Where is Friday and Little Saturday?' she cried.

'I gave them each a herby pasty[3], and sent them to Windmill with grist to grind for to-morrow's baking,' answered the witch, spreading her petticoats over the dark water of the well.

'Tired as I am, I must go to Windmill to look for my dear children,' said the poor Little Mother, with a sigh. 'P'r'aps I shall meet them coming back; and up the lane she went on her way out to Windmill.

When she came back to the well the old witch had smoked her pipe, and was sound asleep and snoring.

'I have been all the way out to Windmill, and I could not see Friday and Little Saturday anywhere,' cried the Little Mother, shaking the old hag roughly by the shoulder. 'Where are they, you wicked old witch?'

'Friday and Little Saturday came back soon after you had gone to look for them,' said the witch, opening her eyes and yawning.

'Where are they?' demanded the Little Mother.

'With Monday, Tuesday, Wednesday, and Thursday,' answered the witch, knocking the ashes out of her pipe.

'And where is Monday and the others?'

'Upstairs,' answered the witch.

'Whose stairs?' asked Betty.

'*My* stairs,' returned the witch.

'Shall I go up your stairs and bring them?' asked the Little Mother eagerly.

'Your shoes are too dirty,' cried the witch.

'I will take off my shoes,' said Betty.

'Your stockings are too dirty,' protested the witch.

'I will take off my stockings.'

'Your feet are too dirty,' protested the old hag.

'I will wash my feet,' said the Little Mother.

'No water would wash them clean enough to climb up my stairs,' cried the witch.

'I'll cut off my feet,' persisted Betty, determined that no excuse should stop her from getting to her children.

'The blood would drop and stain my stairs,' said the witch.

'I'll tie up my stumps,' cried the Little Mother.

'The blood would come through,' howled the witch.

'Then, what shall I do to get up your stairs?' said the Little Mother, with a cry of despair.

'*Fly up!*' cackled the old hag.

'But I can't fly without wings,' wailed Betty.

'Get wings,' cried the witch, with a sneer.

'How can I?' asked the poor Little Mother helplessly.

'I leave that to your clever wits to find out!' snapped the witch. 'And let me tell you that until you *can* fly you will never see Monday and your five other children again, nor get them out of my clutches!' And with a 'Ha! ha!' and a 'He! he!' the witch pulled her petticoats round her and disappeared under the dark waters of the well.

'My dear life!' ejaculated Betty, now really frightened. 'I believe that old woman who played the game with us was a *real* witch, and wasn't pretending at all, and has really and truly taken Monday, Tuesday, and all the others away.' And she sped away down to the quay where she lived with her terrible news.

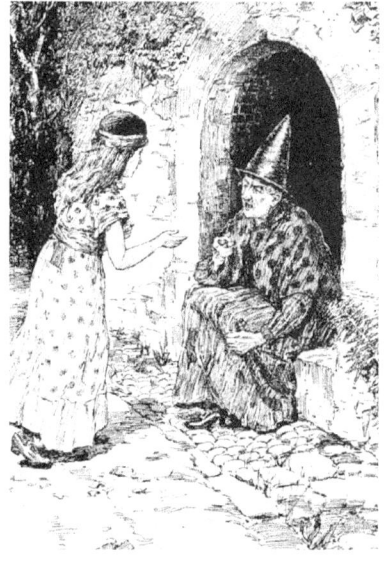

'"Fly up!" cackled the old hag.'

There was a great to-do when the children's friends learned what had happened, and there was bitter woe and lamentation when, after days and days of searching, the poor little souls could not be found.

A year went by, and all this time Betty, the child who had acted the 'Mother' in the game, never forgot her six little friends. They were seldom out of her thoughts, and she longed for a pair of wings to fly up the witch's stairs; and the more she wanted wings, the more impossible they seemed to get.

One evening in the beginning of June—the very same day, as it happened, that she and her little companions had met together at the Witch's Well to play the game—she was passing the well, when a little white dog ran out of a garden close by, and came and licked her shoes.

She was fond of dogs, and, as she patted it, to her amazement it began to talk to her just like a human being, which almost scared her out of her wits.

'Please don't be afraid of me,' he said, wagging his stump of a tail as Betty backed into the hedge. 'I am only a dog in shape. I was a little boy before the dreadful old Witch o' the Well turned me into a dog, or what looks like a dog.'

'Were you really a boy once? And do you know the Witch o' the Well?' asked Betty, trying to get over her fears in her interest in what he told her.

'Alas, I do!' answered the dog. 'She is my mistress, and I have to follow her about all day long, and am never free of her except at night, when she is riding about on her broom. Then I have to haunt certain lanes to make silly superstitious people believe I am a ghost. The old Witch sent me to this lane a few days ago, and very glad I was, because I hoped to see you.'

'Whatever for?' asked Betty, still very much afraid of this strange dog, with his human-like voice.

'Because I know your little friends Monday and the others.'

'Do you really?' cried the child. 'I *am* glad!—Where are they?'

'In the witch's house, away on a dark moor, in her upstairs chamber,' answered the little white dog, with a wag of his tail, 'and where they will have to stay—so the witch says—until the little maid who played "Mother" in the game is able to fly upstairs after them.'

'Then, I'm afraid they will have to stay there always,' said Betty, her eyes filling with tears. 'Can't you get up the witch's stairs and bring them down?'

'The stairs are almost as steep as a tower,' answered the dog; 'and even if I could climb them, the door of the chamber where they are shut up is locked, and a spell worked upon the lock that nothing can open save a pair of wings and music.'

'What kind of music?' asked Betty.

'I haven't the smallest idea,' answered the dog. 'I only know that it has to do with you.'

'Are my dear little friends happy?' asked Betty, hardly noticing the dog's last remark.

'They are most unhappy,' said the dog. 'They have nothing to cheer them, poor little souls, save the forlorn hope that perhaps one day their dear Little Mother Betty will be able to fly and get them out of the witch's power.'

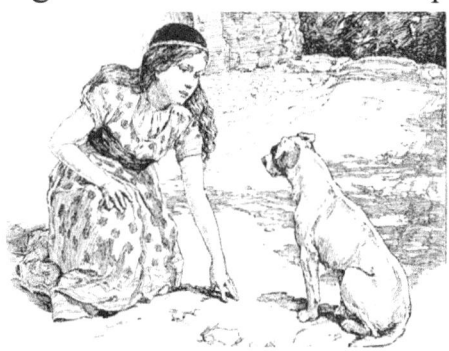

'The little white dog seemed to bend his head in thought.'

'If I only knew how to fly, how quickly I would get up those stairs!' said Betty. 'There is nothing I can do, is there, to get a pair of wings?' she asked wistfully. 'Nobody who can help me to get wings?' she added, as the little white dog seemed to bend his head in thought.

'Nobody but the Wise Woman of Bogee Down,' he answered, after considering a few minutes.

'I have heard of that strange old body,' said Betty. 'My mother often told me about her. She is very clever and wise, she said, and used to make simples for sick folks. She is terribly old now—a hundred and twenty, I think she told me.'

'That or more,' said the dog. 'But aged as she is, she is not too aged to work a kindness for anybody that asks her, particularly if it be against the Witch o' the Well.'

'Will she help me to get wings, do you think?' asked Betty eagerly.

'If it is within her power, I am certain she will,' returned the little white dog. 'Why don't you go and see her, and tell her the old Witch o' the Well has shut up six dear little maids, who were unfortunate enough to play the game with her a year ago, and that they cannot be set free until you, who acted the "Mother" in the game, can *fly* up to their rescue?'

''Tis a long way to Bogee Down,' answered Betty, 'but I'll go there to-morrow, all the same, if I can.'

'That is well,' cried the little white dog. 'You will not seek her help in vain, I am sure, especially if you tell her the witch's little white dog Pincher sent you. Now I must be off, for the old witch is up on her broom, and if she should happen to see us talking together, her horrid old cat would sclow[4] our eyes out. Good-bye, dear little Betty, and give thee favour in the sight of the Wise Woman'; and with another wag of his tail he vanished.

Betty hardly slept a wink that night, thinking of her six little friends shut up in the witch's tower, and so ardently did she desire wings to fly up to their help that she got up and dressed before the sun was risen. He was just rising over the golden towans on the east side of the river as she left her mother's house for Bogee Down, a wild, picturesque, but lonely tableland about four miles from the ancient town.

It was so early that nobody was up except herself, and the doors of the Crown and Anchor were still closed as she walked over the quay, down the slip, and across the beach to the south quay.

The child went out of the town the nearest way to the downs, up through a side road called the Drang, and up Sander's Hill.

When she got up to Three Turnings, which commanded a view of the river and Padstow low in the hollow of the hills, she climbed a stile and looked down to see if she could see the quay.

The river was now very beautiful with reflections of the dawn, and its pale-blue water was flushed with tenderest rose and gold. There was a flush on the rounded hills, and a gleam of light on the distant tors—Rough Tor and Brown Willy. There was a ship in full sail coming up the harbour, followed by a company of white-breasted gulls, which also caught the light.

The sun was high in the sky when Betty reached Bogee Down. Now she had got there she did not know in what part of it the Wise Woman lived. As she sent her glance over the wild down, gorgeous with yellow broom and other down flowers, she thought she saw blue smoke rising from a hedge a short distance up from Music Water, a delightful spot where Sweet-Gales, Butterfly Orchises, Bog-Asphodels grew, and where a clear brown musical stream ran down between the fragrant flowers, which made the place that June morning very beautiful.

The child went up over the down where she had seen the smoke rising, and found a hut huddled under a high blackberry hedge.

She knocked at the door, which was half open, and a thin cracked voice called out:

'Come in and tell me what has brought thee to this lonely down.'

Betty obeyed, but not without fear; and as she pushed the door open, she saw sitting in front of a peat fire on the hearthstone the bent form of an old woman with her back to the door. She was quaintly dressed, after the manner of ancient dames of the sixteenth century, and on her head she wore a cap as white as sloe blossom.

The old dame did not look round as Betty entered, but when the child had said all that Pincher the little white dog had told her to say, and had asked if she would kindly help her to get wings to fly up the witch's stairs, she suddenly glanced at her over her shoulder, with the brightest, keenest eyes the girl had ever seen, and which seemed to look into her pure young soul.

Evidently Betty's earnest little face pleased her, for she smiled and said kindly:

'Pincher was a wise dog to send you to me. But, let me tell you, you have asked me to do an almost impossible thing. Yet, fortunately for those poor shut-up little maids, it is not quite impossible; but it will depend on yourself, whether your love and pity for your little friends is strong enough to do all that is required of you.'

'I'll do *anything* if I can only get wings to fly with, and see Monday, Tuesday, and the others again,' broke in Betty, with all a child's eagerness.

'Alas! the will that is strong and eager to do is often weakened by the flesh that is frail,' said the Wise Woman, with a shake of her head; 'but the question now is, Are you willing to live with me, an old woman, in this out-of-the-way place, for a year and a day, if 'tis required, and do all I bid you willingly, without asking a single question?'

'A year and a day is a long time to be away from home,' said Betty honestly. 'Still, I am willing to stay with you all that time and do your bidding if my mother will let me.'

'That is well!' cried the Wise Woman. 'Now go back to Padstow Town and get your mother's consent, and return to me to-morrow about this time.'

Betty's mother was very glad to let her little girl go and live with the Wise Woman, for she was very poor, and had twelve children.

The next day, when Betty was returning to Bogee Down, which she did by the same road as before, with her clothes done up in a bundle under her arm, who should she see, leaning over a gate, at a place called Uncle Kit's Corner, but the old Witch o' the Well, smoking her pipe!

'Whither away, my little dear?' cried the witch, as the child drew near the gate.

154

'To get a pair of wings to fly up your stairs to see Monday and the others,' answered Betty promptly.

'Ha! ha! That's too funny!' cried the witch. 'As well try to cut a piece from the blue of yon sky to make yourself a gown as to get wings to fly up my stairs.' And she laughed and laughed until she nearly choked herself.

'The witch may crow like an evil bird now,' cried the Wise Woman when Betty told her what the witch had said; 'but I shall hope to live to hear her screech like a whitnick[5] before that time has passed.'

When the little maid had undone her bundle, and put away her small belongings, the old woman told her to go to the settle, which stood by the fireplace, and take out from its seat a little bag of feathers, and separate one from the other and lay them on the table.

'That will be an easy thing to do,' said Betty to herself; and lifting the seat, she found a dinky bag stuffed full of feathers, rainbow-coloured, but so matted together that they were nothing but a soft ball.

'P'r'aps this is to make me a pair of wings,' said Betty; and seating herself on the settle, she set to work with a will.

But the feathers were not easily disentangled, as she soon found, and when evening came she had only succeeded in disentangling one tiny feather from the matted mass.

The Wise Woman neither looked nor spoke to her until the sun sank down behind the downs, when she told her to return the bag to its place in the settle, and then get her supper and her own and go to bed.

'I have only got *one* little feather to put on the table,' said poor little Betty, when she had put the bag back into its place.

'You have done better than I feared,' said the Wise Woman quietly. 'It is something to have untangled even *one* feather from its companions. It is a sign that it is quite possible that you may be able to fly.'

When they had had their supper, which consisted of black bread and goat's milk, Betty lay down in a bed made of dried grass and bracken, in the corner of the room, and slept the sleep of well-doing.

'It will take me a whole year to untangle all these feathers,' said the little maid to herself the next day, when she again sat down to her task, which she did when she had got her own and the Wise Woman's breakfast, and had swept and sanded the hut. ''Tis dreary work, sure 'nough!'

'Pity, love, and patience will do wonders,' said the Wise Woman, who seemed to have the gift of thought-reading, and what she said comforted the child not a little.

Every day for six long months Betty sat in the settle most of the day separating feather from feather, and it was not until the end of that time that the last feather was laid upon the table, and so bright and beautiful did they look that she said they looked as if they had been dipped in a rainbow.

The Wise Woman did not tell her what they were for, but she was sure they were to make her a pair of wings. 'And how beautiful they will be when they are made—brighter than a sunset!' she whispered to herself as she lay down to sleep that night.

When Betty awoke the following morning, she looked at the table to see if the feathers were safe, and saw, to her dismay, the Wise Woman sweep them into the skirt of her gown and take them to the door and shake them out on the down.

'Aw, my beautiful feathers!' ejaculated the child, springing up in her bed, when as she did so the ancient dame broke into a chant, and all she could make out of it was that now the spell was broken they must go with all speed to the Queen of the Little People and get her permission to help in the undoing of another spell.

When the chant had ceased, Betty, still more amazed, saw a great cloud, that looked more like winged flowers than feathers, float away over the downs towards the sea.

'I don't believe they were feathers at all!' cried Betty to herself. 'And, aw dear! how am I to get my wings *now*?'

She longed to ask the Wise Woman to tell her why she had flung the feathers away, but remembering what the old body had said, that she was to ask no questions, whatever she saw or heard, she kept back the words on her lips.

She was very cast down when her work of many days was gone—she knew not whither.

When she had had her breakfast and had done all her little chores, the Wise Woman bade her search in the seat of the settle for a black stone, which, she told her, she must rub till it was the colour of life.

After much searching, she found the stone of curious shape wrapped in soft leather, which her old friend said she could use to rub the stone with.

Betty again set to work with a will, but rub as hard as she could, no rubbing seemed to affect the blackness of the stone, and at the end of a week it seemed *blacker* than ever. She was much troubled at this, and the Wise Woman, who read her thoughts, told her not to despair, as its blacker blackness was a sign that all would be well, and that she was in a fair way of getting wings to fly up the witch's stairs.

'How?' was on Betty's lips, but a warning look from the Wise Woman's wonderful bright eyes made the question die unspoken.

For many a week longer the girl rubbed the sable stone—patiently and quietly most of the time, but there were days when she felt like throwing the stone out of the window and running away home to her mother. But pity for her poor little friends shut up in the witch's chamber made her persevere with her task.

One day, when she was almost worn out with rubbing, she saw a faint glow come into the stone, which, as she rubbed harder and quicker than ever, grew brighter and brighter, until it lay in her hand as red as a poppy.

'The stone is all afire!' she cried, taking it to the Wise Woman.

'It is the colour of life at last,' said the ancient dame, gazing at it with her wonderful bright eyes; 'and another spell loosened to the witch's undoing,' she muttered, half to herself. And noticing that Betty was listening with all her ears, she told the child to look in the settle for a box, and when she had found it to put it on the table and lay the stone within it.

There was only one box in the settle, which, though small, was most exquisitely carved all over with wings—wing interlacing wing—and as Betty set it on the table and put the stone into it, she thought she had never seen such a lovely box.

The next morning, when she awoke, she saw the Wise Woman at the door of the hut with the stone in her hand, and she heard her chanting: 'Go the way thy sisters went—the way of the west wind, and ask the King of the Wee Folk to give thee permission to help in the undoing of an evil wrought by the Witch o' the Well;' and Betty, staring with all her eyes, saw the ancient dame fling the stone out on to the down, along which it rolled at a rapid rate, burning as it went with a rosy splendour. It went the way the feathers had gone.

Betty dressed quickly, and busied herself about the hut, to keep herself from asking if the stone was really a stone, for she did not believe it was, and she ached to know.

When they had had breakfast, and the hut was cleaned with fresh scouring-sand, the Wise Woman asked her, if she had the chance of being made into a bird, what little bird would she like to be.

'A thrush,' said Betty. 'I should love to be a little thrush, because it sings so sweetly in the dawn.'

'It is a good choice,' cried the Wise Woman—'the best you could have made. Now go down to Trevillador Wood, and every thrush you see in it, ask him to give you a feather for Love's sake.'

'I do not know where Trevillador Wood is,' said the child, 'nor the way thither.'

'It is in a valley in Little Petherick,' returned the Wise Woman. 'It is not a great way from here, and easy to find if you follow a little brown stream from Crackrattle, that runs down through the valley to the wood. Crackrattle is away there, on Trevibban Down,' pointing to the opposite down, which was only separated from Bogee by a narrow road. 'By going up across Trevibban you will soon get to Crackrattle. Now go, my dear, and go quickly.' And Betty went.

The child was ever so thankful to be out of doors again, after having been cooped up in the hut for so many months, particularly as it was the birds' singing-time. Birds were singing everywhere on the downs, and their music gushed from furze-brake, from thorn-bush and alder; and when she came to Music Water she heard linnets fluting, and sweet wild notes came from budding willows by the side of the rippling stream. Larks were also singing—lark answering lark with such wonderful melody in the blue upper air that she told herself she had never heard such lovely sounds before.

The downs, in spite of all the bird-music, were not so beautiful nor so full of colour as when she came to stay with the Wise Woman. They were now as brown as Piskey-purses, she said, and only lightened here and there by granite boulders, where they caught the rays of the sun, by yellow gorse, and splashes of silver lichen.

It did not take the girl very long to cross Music Water's full stream to reach the road that parted the two downs; but it took her some time to get to Crackrattle, as the way up to it was thick with brambles and furze.

When she drew near that part of the down which commanded a grand view of the country and sea as far up as Tintagel, she turned her gaze towards Padstow Town, and saw the river twisting in and out of the hills on its way out to the open sea. She also saw the two great headlands, Stepper Point and Pentire, that guarded the entrance to Padstow harbour in that far-away sixteenth century, as they do to-day, and her glimpse of them and the blue river seemed to bring her home quite close to her; and when she reached Crackrattle stream, she followed it down the long, deep valley with a happy heart.

When she came to a wood, which she was sure in her mind was Trevillador Wood, she heard the thrushes singing and filling the place with music. Every cock thrush was doing his very best to out-sing his brother thrush. It was mating-time, and each little songster in speckled grey was trying to win a little mate by his song.

The first thrush that Betty saw—and he was a master singer and made the wood ring—was on the uppermost branch of a horse-chestnut just beginning to bud, and when he had finished his entrancing song, she lifted up her voice and said:

'Dear little grey thrush, please give me one of your feathers, for *Love's* sake.'

She wondered as she begged if the bird would understand her language; but he did quite well, and, what she thought was still more wonderful, she understood his!

'I will give you a feather gladly,' he piped in his own delicious thrush way. 'It is the beautiful spring-time, and the thrushes' courting-time; and because you beg a feather for *Love's* sake, I will pluck one that lies over my heart.' And the dear little bird did so, and flung it down into Betty's outstretched hands; and when she had caught it, he burst out into exquisite melody, and he was still singing, as she went down the wood lovely with budding trees.

From every thrush she saw she asked a feather for *Love's* sake, and she was not refused once, and by the time she had gone the length of the wood her apron was full of thrushes' feathers, plucked from breast and wing, tail and back!

'Were the song-thrushes willing to give their feathers?' asked the Wise Woman when Betty got back to the hut.

'Ever so willing!' cried the little maid, opening her apron to show what a lot she had got.

'It is more than enough,' she said. 'Put them into the box where the stone lay.'

The following morning when the child awoke there was a mournful sound coming up from the sea, which they could command from the door of the hut, and the Wise Woman said it was a sign that a great storm was being brewed by the Master of the Winds, and that before the day was over he would send the great North-Easter across the land.

'I am sorry,' she said, 'as it will hinder our work, and perhaps I shall die of the cold before we can help you to fly.'

Betty wanted terribly to ask the Wise Woman who beside herself would help her to get wings, but she dared not ask a single question, and felt it was very hard she could not.

Before the day had closed in, the bitter north wind, which was accompanied by snow, had come. It broke over the downs in great fury, and made the poor old woman shiver over her fire with the misery of it. The next day and the next it blew, and the more it blew, and the faster it snowed, the more the ancient dame shivered and shook; and all day long she kept Betty busy piling up dry furze on the hearth, till there was none left to put.

When she realized that all her winter store of peat and firewood was burnt, she moaned, and said she was sure she should die of the cold.

'And if I die,' she added sadly, 'the witch, like the north wind, will have it all her own way, and you will never be able to fly up her terrible stairs.'

This distressed the poor little maid very much; for she had become quite fond of the Wise Woman, and wanted her to live for her own sake as well as for Monday's, Tuesday's, and the others'.

When the fuel was all burnt, and the Wise Woman too cold even to shiver, Betty said that when it stopped snowing she would go out on the downs and look for something to burn; and when it stopped she went.

The downs were many feet deep under the snow, and there was not a furze-brake nor a hillock to be seen anywhere; and the down opposite was as smooth as a sheet spread out on grass to dry.

As Betty was searching for wood, and could not find even a stick, a hare came speeding over the snow from Crackrattle. She watched it till it crossed over to Bogee, and saw, to her surprise, that it was making straight for her. When it drew near it stopped, with eyes that made her think of the witch's eyes, and as it gazed, the hare disappeared, and in its place stood the old witch herself, steeple-hat and all!

Betty was dreadfully frightened, and before she could rush back to the hut, the witch had come quite close to her, and asked her what she was doing out there in the cold.

'Looking for firewood for the poor old Wise Woman's fire,' answered Betty. 'And I can't see any,' she added sadly.

'Of course you can't,' laughed the witch. 'Sticks under three feet of snow are as difficult to find as a furze-needle in a wainload of hay. It will comfort you to know that you won't find even a stick, and that before the north wind has turned his back on the downs, the Wise Woman will have died of the cold, and you will cry your eyes out for wings to fly up my stairs!' And cackling and jeering, she disappeared, and Betty saw a gray hare running away over the snow down to Music Water, now as silent as the downs themselves.

The little maid was returning to the hut with an icicle of despair at her heart, when a white dog ran across her path, and looking down, she saw it was Pincher, the witch's dog.

'Don't let what my bad old mistress said distress you,' he cried, licking Betty's cold little hand. 'She does not want you to look for sticks, and came here on purpose to prevent you. She is quite as anxious that the Wise Woman should die as you and I are for her to live. She is as clever as she is vile, and she knows that a woman over a hundred could not possibly live long in awful weather like this unless she has a good fire to keep her warm.'

'But why does she want the Wise Woman to die?' asked the little maid.

'Because she fears the wisdom of her long years can help you to fly up her stairs. And this fear brought her to Bogee Down to-day. She made me come with her, which is fortunate; for poking about whilst she was talking to you, I discovered a great faggot of wood dry as a bone, and under it a pile of peat.'

'Where?' Betty asked eagerly.

'Close to the hut under a hedge,' answered the dog. 'And if you will allow me I'll come and help you to get it out. The witch is so happy in her belief that she has discouraged you from looking for sticks that she won't miss me yet.'

And he led the way to the side of the hut, where, under a tangle of brambles, Betty saw a huge bundle of sticks, dry and brown.

They set to work with a will—she with her eager young hands, he with his strong white teeth—and soon got it out from under the hedge and into the hut, where, to their distress, they found the Wise Woman lying face down on the hearthstone, apparently lifeless.

Betty, girl-like, began to sob, believing the poor old woman was dead, which made Pincher quite angry, and he told her with a growl to put off her weeping till a more convenient time, and see if she could not kindle a fire with the sticks they had brought, whilst he tried to lick life back into her poor old body.

It was just the stimulus the child wanted. She mopped away her tears, and piled wood on the fire and set it alight; and Pincher, the dog, licked the poor old woman's face and hands with his warm, moist tongue.

Their efforts were not in vain, and they soon had the joy of seeing her open her eyes and stretch out her hands to the blaze.

'Thank you for all your kindness, dear Pincher,' said Betty, when the dog said he must go. 'If I can ever do you a kindness in return, just ask me and I'll do it if I can.'

'Remember me when you can fly up the witch's stairs,' said the dog, with an appealing look in his eyes that Betty never forgot.

'Then you really believe I shall be able to fly up those stairs some day?' she asked.

'I am almost certain you will, and so is the witch. You cannot live with people for generations without being able to read their faces. The witch's face is an open book to me now, and it tells me that she is not only afraid you will fly, but that it will happen soon. So fearful is she of this that a few days ago she actually wove another spell on the door leading up to the tower where the little maids who played the game are kept.'

'Do you ever get mouth-speech with the poor little dears?' asked Betty wistfully.

'Never. But I sometimes see them at the barred window of their chamber. It isn't often they have time even for that, for the old witch keeps them spinning all day long. Farewell, dear! I *must* go. If the faggot of sticks is all burnt and the turf before the cold goes, don't go out again in search of more firewood. There is danger abroad. If the Wise Woman is in danger of sinking under the cold, just lay your warm heart against her heart, and all will be well.'

The dreadful weather still continued, and when the faggot was all burnt, the dame again began to shiver and shake with cold, and said she should die this time, as there was no warmth left to keep life in her.

Betty was once more greatly distressed on her old friend's account, and declared she would go out on the downs to look for firewood in spite of what might happen to herself; but as she was going, the Wise Woman again tumbled, face down, on the fireless hearth.

As the girl picked her up (she was not the weight of a witch) and laid her on the settle, she remembered what the dog had advised her to do if the cold overcame the old woman again, and, lying down beside her, she pressed her warm young body against her aged body, and soon she had the joy of knowing that life was creeping back to the feeble old frame.

When the Wise Woman opened her eyes and saw the child's face close to hers, and felt her kind young arms about her, she said, with a tremble in her voice:

'Thou art a dear little maid. Thou hast rekindled the feeble flame of my life, proving to me that Good is greater than Evil, and Love stronger than Hate. I shall not die now before thou hast gotten thy wings. Get up, open the door, and call across the snow three times, "Little Prince Fire, come away from the Small People's Country and keep the Wise Woman warm till the cold goes!"'

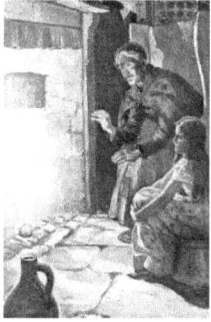

'The stone was on the hearthstone, burning away like a faggot.'

Betty made haste to obey, and when she had opened the hut-door wide she called three times, as she was told, and then waited to see what would happen.

In a minute or less there appeared on the edge of the down a bright-red glow like a poppy in the eye of the sun. After burning there a minute or so it came like a flash over the snow towards the hut. As it came close, she saw it was the very same stone that she had rubbed for so many, many weeks.

It flashed like a ruby into the hut, and as it did so she thought she saw, through the soft rosy haze that seemed to envelope it, a tiny laughing face.

When she turned to see where the stone had gone, behold it was on the hearthstone, burning away like a tiny faggot, and the Wise Woman was sitting beside it with her withered old hands held out to the blaze!

It was so remarkable and queer that Betty could not at first believe the evidence of her own eyes, and rubbed them to make sure she was not dreaming. But it was no dream, for the miserable little hut, which a few minutes before was cold as Greenland, was now as warm as a zam[6] oven, and there was a soft glow all over it.

She sat down on the settle to enjoy the comfort of this wonderful fire, and she felt so warm and lovely after the terrible cold that it made her drowsy, and in a little while she was in a sound sleep. She never knew how long she slept, she only knew that when she awoke the wind and the snow had all gone, and the down birds were chanting a morning song outside the window. The stone was also gone, and the Wise Woman nowhere to be seen.

As she was wondering what had become of the latter, the old woman came into the hut with her apron full of green furze, and seeing the child wide awake, she cried:

'Get up, sleepy-head! The cold has left the downs this longful time, and the thrushes in Trevillador Wood have built their nests and are beginning to lay. Haste to the wood and get a bottleful of bird-music.'

'Where is the bottle?' asked Betty, getting up and looking about her.

'You will find one in the settle made of the Small People's crystal, into which you must ask every thrush you hear singing to his mate to drop a note to make a song with. Ask him to give it you for *Gratitude's* sake. When the bottle is full to its neck make your way back to the hut, and the first living thing you see after you have left the wood ask it to return with you to the Wise Woman. Ask it also to come for Gratitude's sake.'

After the child had eaten some food and had found the bottle, which was ever so tiny, and clear and bright as diamonds, she started for Trevillador Wood.

The cold had indeed all gone, as the Wise Woman had said, and the downs were all the better for the great storm that had swept over them. The snow had kept the earth warm, and had been a soft warm blanket to all the downflowers, and now the furze blossom was all manner of lovely shades of gold, and the soft spring air full of its fragrance. Music Water was all alight with marsh-marigolds, and the catkins of the grey-green willows were dusted with gold.

The snow had also been kind to the trees in Trevillador Wood (the Thrushes' Wood, Betty called it), and had wrapped all the baby buds and tender leaves in dainty white furs, and when the little maid entered the wood she saw, to her surprise, that most of the trees were dreams of beauty, with glistering leaves, and some of them were almost as brightly coloured as that strange stone, Little Prince Fire, as the Wise Woman had called it.

So delighted was she with all she saw that she forgot what she had been sent there for, until a thrush near startled the wood with a burst of melody. He was singing to his mate, for, drawing nearer, she saw, low down in a bush, a little hen thrush on her nest.

'Please, little grey-bird[7], will you drop a note of your song into this bottle for *Gratitude's* sake?' she asked, holding up the bottle to the singing thrush.

'Gladly,' piped he, 'especially as you ask it for Gratitude's sake. We have just received our first great blessing, which I may tell you is a tiny blue egg.'

'Give the child *two* notes,' piped a happy little voice from the nest. 'My heart is brimming over with joy for the warm wee thing under me.'

'Thank you for your kindness,' said Betty. 'But, if you please, little thrushes, the Wise Woman who lives on Bogee Down above Music Water, who sent me to this wood, said I must only ask for *one* note from each thrush I heard singing.'

'That is right,' chirped the little cock thrush. 'Always obey those older and wiser than yourself.'

'Ask the child what she wants thrushes' notes for,' chirped the voice from the nest. 'She didn't say, did she?'

'I forgot to tell you that,' struck in Betty. 'It is to make a song with.'

'I thought so,' piped the little cock thrush, and flying down, he put one of his most delicious notes into the tiny bottle, and in another second he was up on his bush again, singing deeper and more entrancingly than before, gratitude being the keynote and the chief utterance of his song.

Betty went down the wood with that music in her soul, and begged every thrush she heard singing to give her a note of his song.

Whether every bird's heart was also full of gladness for the freckled blue eggs in its dear little nest we cannot say, but they all gave willingly of their best, and before the child had gone through Trevillador Wood, the bottle of Small People's crystal was full to the neck with thrush-music.

Coming back, she saw two red squirrels sitting on their haunches at the foot of an oak-tree, eating nuts.

Said one squirrel to the other squirrel:

'There is a dear little maid from Padstow Town here in the wood collecting music from the thrushes. It is the same child who, unknown to herself, undid a cruel spell which the Witch o' the Well cast over Prince Fire, a near relative of the King of the Little People. She turned him into a black stone, and a stone he had to be till somebody could rub it the colour of flame.'

'You don't mean to say so?' cried the other squirrel. 'This *is* news.'

'I thought it would be,' said the squirrel that spoke, arching his handsome tail with importance. 'Perhaps it will also be news to you to hear that this same little maid has actually untangled the dear Little Lady Soft Winds from that great Skein of Entanglement into which the wicked old witch tangled them, and from which nobody, not even the Wee Folk themselves, was able to free them.'

'However did she manage to do it?' asked the second squirrel.

'Only the Wise Woman of Bogee Down could answer *that* question. But the thrushes believe, and so do I, that love and pity for six little maids whom the witch has shut up somewhere gave patience to her fingers to do what the Wise Woman bade her do; and because her heart was full of love for these poor little maids, whom she hoped by her obedience to get out of the witch's power, she unwittingly set free the other poor little prisoners—the Lady Soft Winds and Prince Fire, the King's cousin.'

'And has she got her own little friends out of the power of the witch after all her love and patience?' asked the squirrel.

'Alas! not yet; but we all hope she will soon. The Small People are her friends now, especially those she set free. And it is told that they are going to turn her into a flying creature of some sort. Some say a bird, but nobody knows for certain. We are all on the alert to see what will happen. They say the Lady Soft Winds whispered to the daffodowndillies last evening that Prince Fire had already begun to make a pair of wings for her to fly up the witch's stairs. But it may be only talk. And yet—there! the dear little maid is coming. Not another word, remember. She understands our language, and bird language too. The Wise Woman, it is said, put something on her tongue when she was asleep one day, when Little Prince Fire came from the Wee Folk's country to keep the Wise Woman's hut warm;' and then, catching sight of Betty's eyes bent upon him, he rushed up the trunk of the oak, followed by his companion.

'Well, those little funny things have told news, sure 'nough,' laughed the child to herself when the pretty little squirrels had vanished, 'and have told me all I ached to know without asking a single question. To think that the little feathers were the dear Little People; and that queer black stone was one too, and that they are going to help me fly up to Monday and the rest!'

And she danced with delight as she thought of it, and the wonder was she did not dance the thrushes' notes out of the bottle.

When she was out of the wood, and walking up to Crackrattle, she remembered what the Wise Woman had told her, that the first thing she saw with wings she must ask it to return with her to the hut; but the only winged creature that she noticed as she went up the valley was a large butterfly—or what she thought was a butterfly—on a great stone.

'The Wise Woman cannot want a butterfly to go back with me to her house,' said Betty to herself. 'But perhaps I had better ask it to come;' and speaking gently, so as not to frighten away the lovely thing on the stone, she said: 'Little butterfly, please will you, for Gratitude's sake, come with me to the Wise Woman's hut?' and to her amazement the tiny creature answered back:

'Gladly will I go with you. But, excuse me, I am not a butterfly. I am one of the Lady Soft Winds whom you freed from the tangle into which the old witch threw us.'

It began to rise on its azure wings as it spoke, and as it rose Betty saw it was indeed a fairy. It had the dearest little face she had ever seen, and as for its eyes, they were bluer than its own wings, and its soft, round cheeks were a more delicate pink than the cross-leaved heath that flowered on the downs early in the summer.

It flew on beside her, and Betty was so taken up with watching it that she did not notice when she got up to Crackrattle that a dozen other fairy-like creatures were flying over the downs towards her, until they were quite close.

'We are the Lady Soft Wind's sisters,' they said, 'and out of deep gratitude to *you* we have come to go with you to the Wise Woman's hut.'

'Have you really, you little dears?' was all Betty could find words to say. 'Come along, then.'

And they came, and were a rhythm of colour as they flew beside her, or, as the child expressed it, 'a little flying garland of flowers.'

Thus accompanied, Betty came to the hut, where, in the doorway, stood the Wise Woman, leaning on her stick, evidently awaiting her and her companions' arrival.

'We have come,' said one of the little creatures.

'I felt certain you would,' said the Wise Woman, making a curtsey, 'and a thousand welcomes. If the child has brought the thrushes' notes everything is ready.'

'She has brought them,' put in another tiny voice, 'and they are impatient to sing.'

'Then please follow me,' said the Wise Woman, going into the hut; and in flew all the lovely little creatures, with gentle fanning of wings, which made a soft breeze as they came.

'Prince Fire is already at work,' said the Wise Woman, pointing to the box, and Betty, who had followed the Little Lady Soft Winds, saw, sitting in the box amongst the thrushes' feathers, a small person dressed in red, busy making wings! He was Little Prince Fire, and a very great person in the Small People's World.

'My dear life! aw, my dear life! What shall I see next?' cried the little Padstow maid to herself; and what more she would have said is not known, for at that moment the Wise Woman took the tiny crystal bottle out of her hand and put it into the box beside the dinky person within.

'The Lady Soft Winds have arrived, your Royal Highness,' she said, 'and Betty, the little Padstow maid, is also here.'

'Good!' piped the tiny man. 'Bid them sing the Making Song.'

'We require no bidding, Prince Fire,' said a little Lady Soft Wind, with gentle dignity, as she and the others alighted on the table. 'Out of gratitude and love we have come from afar to sing this song, knowing well, unless we sang it, you would never complete the wings. We, as well as you, can never repay the little maid of Padstow Town for releasing us from the witch's spell.'

The voice had hardly died away when all the radiant fairies began to wave their wings, at first slowly, and then rapidly, in a kind of rhythm, and sang very softly as they waved them.

Betty watched them with all her eyes, and whether it was the movement of their wings or the curious song they sang, with its hush-a-by kind of tune, she felt ever so drowsy, just as she had felt when Little Prince Fire blazed away like a faggot on the hearthstone, and sitting down on the settle, she fell asleep with the two first verses of the song in her ears:

'We Wee Folk together
With music and feather
The gift of the birds—
The little grey-birds—
Do make her a thrush
All sweetness and gush.
Lallaby! Gallady!
'And the Little Prince Fire
Her sweet song will inspire,
That she may fly high
Where little maids sigh,
And undo the spell
Of the Witch o' the Well.
Lallaby! Gallady!'

The next thing she heard was the Wise Woman telling her to rise up and move her wings, and Betty, nothing loth, lifted herself from the settle and found she was all air and lightness, like the Little Lady Soft Winds themselves, and could fly about the hut with the greatest ease; the feeling of flying was altogether delightful!

The Lady Soft Winds watched her flight with the deepest interest, and Prince Fire, who was sitting on the edge of the carved box, watched too; that he approved of her flying powers it was plain to see, for his bright eyes never left her wings.

'What am I now?' asked Betty at last, perching on a beam, and looking down sideways bird fashion on the Wise Woman.

'You are a little grey thrush,' said the Wise Woman, her withered face a big smile.

'And now, little grey thrush, away to the east, where the witch's house looms out dark and strong against the gold of the morning sky,' said the Lady Soft Winds, 'and fly up her terrible stairs and set your six little children free, as you did us.'

'Yes; away to Monday, Tuesday, and Wednesday,' cried Little Prince Fire.

'And Thursday, Friday, and Little Saturday,' struck in the Wise Woman.

'Away, away, little grey thrush!' cried they all, singing as they cried. 'The sun is rising behind the Tors, and the time is come for *our* little thrush to fly and sing. Then, away, away!'

Their little thrush wanted no further urging, and with one full, clear, melodious note, which filled all the small fairies with delight, it flew out of the hut, followed by the gentle winnowing of the Lady Soft Winds' wings.

So glad was Betty, the little grey thrush, at being on her way to see those dear little maids that she flew faster than ever thrush flew before, and the sun was not yet over the Tors when she reached a grim old house standing all alone on a brown and desolate moor, with its back to the golden sunrise.

Instinct told the little grey thrush that it was the witch's house, and alighting on a blasted tree, close to its spell-bound door, she began to sing with all her might; and so joyous and so triumphant was her song that it seemed to bring gladness and hope even to that desolate spot.

As Betty, in her bird form, sang on, the old witch came round the corner of her house, dragging her unwilling feet as she came. When she lifted her bad old eyes and saw a grey thrush high on the tree, singing with all its cheerful heart, she turned green, and hearing the door of the tower leading up the stairs—where Monday and all the other little maids were shut up—groaning as if in pain, she sank in a heap on the ground, and began to groan and moan too.

The bird sang on, and its whole body was one shake with its music, and the more thrilling was its song, the more the witch moaned and groaned. Then, when its last triumphant note rang out, the great door opened, as if pushed back by some magic power, and revealed a flight of very steep stairs. The witch gave a piercing howl when she saw the door open wide, for she knew that the small grey thrush's music had broken her spells, and that she was completely in the power of that little singing bird.

When the door of the tower was as wide open as it could go, the thrush gave three flaps of its wings, and then it flew out of the tree, and in through the doorway of the tower, up and up the witch's stairs. And at the top of the stairs was a small room, where six little maids sat spinning.

They were so busy, and the hum of the wheels was so loud, that none of them noticed the entrance of the grey-bird until it broke into a song from the window-sill.

'Why, it is a dear little thrush!' cried Friday, who was the first to notice it. 'How ever *did* it get up here? It must be the bird we heard singing so beautifully outside just now;' and all the children stopped their spinning-wheels to look at it.

'Did it really fly up the witch's stairs?' asked Thursday, resting her sad, soft eyes on the thrush, whose heart was beating so against its speckled breast at the sight of those dear little maids that it couldn't tell them at first who it was.

'It did,' answered Monday, 'and its flying up here makes me think of our Little Mother Betty, who played the game with us. Will she ever be able to fly up the witch's stairs, I wonder?'

'I am afraid not,' said one of the other children, with a sigh. 'I have given up all hope of her ever doing that now.'

'You are wrong, my dears,' cried the thrush, finding its voice at last. 'I am Mother Betty, turned into a dinky bird for your sakes, and have flown up the witch's stairs!'

And it flapped its wings, jerked its tail, and behaved altogether in a most extraordinary manner, for the children's faces of amazement and hope nearly sent it mad with joy. And then, as if it must relieve its feelings still more, it burst into a most enchanting song, which was answered outside the tower by a series of joyful barks from Pincher, the witch's dog.

'It *must* be Little Mother Betty,' said Monday, leaving her spinning-wheel. 'I can hear her own voice in the song.'

Then all the other little maids left their wheels to gaze at the bird.

'Are you *really* Betty who played the "Witch in the Well" with us that terrible day?' they asked.

'Indeed I am,' sang the thrush. 'I have come to take you away from here. Now follow me down the stairs and out of the house.'

'The stairs are so steep,' began Saturday, with frightened eyes.

'Don't be afraid, dear little Saturday,' sang the bird. 'It will be as easy as thinking. Come along, all of you.'

The six little maids followed the bird out of the room and down those wall-like stairs, and in a minute or less were outside the witch's house, where they found the old hag in the act of mounting her broom.

They were met at the door by Pincher the dog, who welcomed them with joyful barks and wagging of tail; and then, finding his mistress had fled, he looked up at the little grey thrush, who was wheeling round and round the children's heads out of sheer gladness, and begged her to give chase to the witch. 'For,' said he, 'if she goes out of your sight before you have commanded her to do something, you are in danger of having to retain your thrush-shape.'

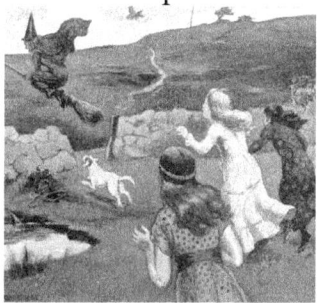

'Over the moor and across the downs they all went.'

'I am glad you told me,' said the thrush, and it was about to fly after the witch, when it recalled to mind what the dog had said the day he helped to drag the faggot of wood into the hut: 'Remember me when you have flown up the witch's stairs.' 'I have been up the witch's stairs and down again,' it said, alighting on the ground beside him. 'Is there anything I can do for you, Pincher? I am here to do it if I can.'

'I long to be set free from the power of the witch,' said the little dog, fixing his gentle eyes on the bird, 'and to be restored to my own shape. If you bid the witch do this, though it will be vinegar and gall to her, she is bound to obey you by the merit of your wings and your song. I long exceedingly to be myself again.'

'You shall,' sang the little grey thrush.

And then, telling the children to mount Footman's Horse[8] and follow hard after her and the witch, it flapped its wings again, and flew after the old hag on her broom, and Pincher the dog and the six little maids sped after them.

Over the moor and across the downs they all went like the wind, the witch keeping well in advance. Uphill and downhill and through the lanes they flew, and never once did they stop till they came to Place Hill, where the great stone gateway of Place House stood greyly out from a background of beech-trees and oaks. Here the six little maids stopped to get breath, but the old hag, though ready to drop from her broom with fatigue, paused not a second, and went on down the hill with little Thrush Betty, and Pincher the dog close behind her.

'The witch is out of sight!' cried Monday, as the old hag and the little grey-bird disappeared round a corner.

'So she is!' said Friday.

And they all whipped up their tired little steeds, and away they sped down the steep hill in pursuit of the witch; but they did not overtake her until she got to the well, when they stood watching to see what would happen.

The old hag slid off her broom, and, looking cunningly about her, as if in search of the thrush, which was on top of the wall above the well, she made a quick step to the well, and put her foot on its ledge.

'Sing, sing, dear Thrush Betty!' cried the small white dog in great distress, or the witch will disappear into the well before you can command her to do what you said.'

And Betty, the little grey-bird, flew into a tree, and began to sing with all its might once more. And as it sang, the old hag crept back from the well, and stood in the middle of the road, with a terrible look on her face.

Now, being a witch, and one of the worst of her kind, she could not endure anything so pure and sweet as the small bird's song; every note it sang was an agony to listen to, and, knowing in her wicked soul that its music had crushed all her evil power, she begged permission in a humble voice to be allowed to go into the well.

'You may go,' sang little Thrush Betty; 'with one condition, which is that you turn Pincher back into a boy!'

'Please ask me something less hard!' pleaded the witch, cringing before the little bird. 'Pincher will be mine no longer if I do that, and I cannot do without my faithful little dog. Where I go, he must also go.'

'That he shall not!' sang the thrush. 'I command you, by the merit of my wings and the power of my song, to remove your spell from this poor little boy!'

'To lose my little white dog is worse than having the Lady Soft Winds and Prince Fire set free from my spells!' muttered the witch. 'Worse even than losing the six little maids who played the game with me and did all my spinning.'

'Give him back his own self this very minute,' sang the little grey thrush, 'or else———'

If a threat was implied in the sentence, the witch understood it, for, with a howl of rage, she made a pass with her broom over the dog. As she did so, the dog vanished, and in its place stood a young boy, dark and very handsome, dressed in clothes of a bygone age!

The six little maids stared at him in open-mouthed astonishment, and as they stared as only little maids can, the witch made for the well.

'Please sing once more, little Thrush Betty,' cried the boy in a voice it knew so well. 'This last song will quite end the power of the bad old witch, and keep her down in the bottom of the Witch's Well until she repents of all she has done.'

'That will be never!' snarled the witch; and with a horrible cry, which even the victorious song of the little grey thrush could not drown, she splashed into the well. And when Monday, Tuesday, and the other little maids could get that cry out of their ears, the well and its quaint old arch were no longer to be seen, and near where it had stood was dear little Betty, their friend, who had played the 'Mother' in the game, looking very little altered, only a few inches taller, and standing beside her, holding her hand, was the boy, who, in his dog-shape, had done so much for them all.

'Now let us go home to our mothers,' cried Friday.

'I have no mother to go to,' said the boy sadly, as he hesitated to go with the happy children. 'Mine died long ago, and I have no home.'

'Our mothers shall be your mother,' cried the little maids, 'and you will never lack anything if you come with us.'

So they all came down through Padstow Town, the boy in their midst.

Nobody noticed them till they reached Middle Street, a straight cobbled street with quaint houses on either side, when a 'Granfer man[9]' spied them, and shouted the news that the long-lost children had come back, and the whole street rushed out to welcome them.

Thursday lived at the bottom of this street, and Betty thought she ought to see her safely home; but the child's mother had already heard of their arrival, and came out to meet them and to clasp her own little maid to her heart.

Monday's home was in a narrow street called Lanedwell, and when she was safe within her parents' house and arms, the other five little maids and the handsome boy, accompanied by a great crowd, went on their way to the market, where Saturday lived.

As they came out of Lanedwell Street, a house across the market stood full in view. It was one of the quaintest of buildings, of Tudor date, with an outside flight of stone stairs leading up to its side entrance under the eaves. Little Saturday's eyes glistened when she caught sight of this house, for it was her own dear home. Her father happened to be at the top of the stairs looking over the wooden rail as the children drew near, and he nearly fell over into the street below when he saw his own long-lost little maid.

Through a narrow passage, called the Blind Entry, the children and crowd of people poured, and they only got through when Saturday's father was down the steps and over to the Entry to greet them.

'There is the "George and the Dragon"!' cried Thursday, pointing to an inn at the bottom of a street as they crossed the market.

'Iss,' said Betty, with a smile; 'and St. George is *still* slaying the Dragon!' gazing up at the sign hanging above the door.

'Perhaps the Dragon is even more difficult to conquer than the Witch o' the Well,' put in the boy, eyeing with great interest the inn's sign, on which was painted in glowing colours England's patron saint, with uplifted sword to slay the Dragon.

'Ever so much more, I reckon,' responded Betty.

Another small street brought them to the quay, where the other four little maids' homes were, as well as Betty's, and to their exceeding joy they saw their fathers and mothers and all their relations and friends coming to meet them. And what a meeting it was, and what a welcome they had!

Never since the day when the two ships, which the people of this ancient town sent fully equipped to help in the siege of Calais in Edward III.'s reign, came safely back was there such rejoicing, so the old 'granfer men[9]' said.

Every vessel in the harbour hoisted its flag in honour of the children's return and the overcoming of that wicked old witch.

The boy, when Betty told how she had got her wings that enabled her to fly up the witch's stairs, was made much of by the people of Padstow Town, and the friends of those seven little maids almost fought who should have him for their own.

How it was settled there is no need to tell, save only that he lived on Padstow quay, and that he and Betty were always friends and loved each other dearly; and when they grew up they married, and were as happy as the summer is long.

1 Bread and cream sprinkled with treacle.

2 Legs.

3 A pasty made of herbs.

4 Scratch.

5 Weasel.

6 A hot oven that has been left to cool a little.

7 The song-thrush is called the grey-bird in Cornwall.

8 Their legs.

9 A *very* old man.

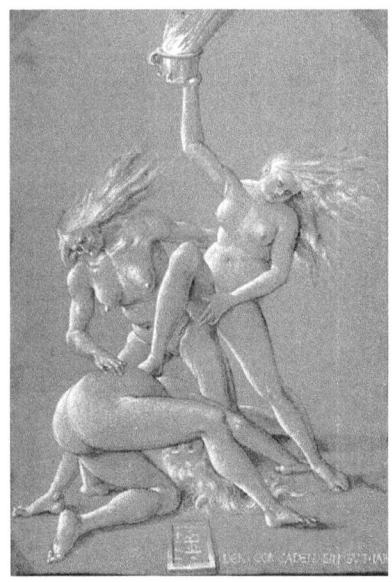